FASTING
FOR
FINANCIAL
BREAK
THROUGH

ELMER L. TOWNS

FASTING
FOR
FINANCIAL
≈BREAK≈
THROUGH

ELMER L. TOWNS

Regal

From Gospel Light
Ventura, California, U.S.A.

Published by Regal Books
From Gospel Light
Ventura, California, U.S.A.
Printed in the U.S.A.

Regal Books is a ministry of Gospel Light, an evangelical Christian publisher dedicated to serving the local church. We believe God's vision for Gospel Light is to provide church leaders with biblical, user-friendly materials that will help them evangelize, disciple and minister to children, youth and families.

It is our prayer that this Regal book will help you discover biblical truth for your own life and help you meet the needs of others. May God richly bless you.

For a free catalog of resources from Regal Books/Gospel Light, please call your Christian supplier or contact us at 1-800-4-GOSPEL *or* www.regalbooks.com.

Cover and interior design by Robert Williams
Edited by Kathi Macias

Library of Congress Cataloging-in-Publication Data
Towns, Elmer L.
    Fasting for financial breakthrough / Elmer Towns.
        p. cm.
Includes bibliographical references.
    ISBN 0-8307-2963-1 (trade paper)
1. Fasting. 2. Money—Religious aspects—Christianity. 3. Finance, Personal—Religious aspects—Christianity. 4. Stewardship, Christian.
I. Title.
    BV5055 .T689 2002
    248.4'7—dc21   2002002369

1 2 3 4 5 6 7 8 9 10 11 12 13 14 15 / 09 08 07 06 05 04 03 02

Rights for publishing this book in other languages are contracted by Gospel Light Worldwide, the international nonprofit ministry of Gospel Light. Gospel Light Worldwide also provides publishing and technical assistance to international publishers dedicated to producing Sunday School and Vacation Bible School curricula and books in the languages of the world. For additional information, visit www.gospellightworldwide.org; write to Gospel Light Worldwide, P.O. Box 3875, Ventura, CA 93006; or send an e-mail to info@gospellightworldwide.org.

CONTENTS

AUTHOR NOTE

Reading this book by itself will give you a narrow view of fasting, and you might walk away thinking that fasting is simply a means to get things like money. Although it is true that fasting is a powerful way to effect breakthrough in financial problems, the primary purpose of prayer and fasting is to know God. Fasting is not about food—it's about meditation, reflection upon the Scriptures and communion with God. If you are just beginning to explore the area of fasting and prayer as a part of your life and you would like a broader perspective on this vital issue, you may want to read my book *Fasting for Spiritual Breakthrough* for a balanced and comprehensive view.

In addition, I want to stress that not everyone should fast from physical food. If you have one of the approximately 30 physical pathologies that require food, you would harm your health if you fasted. God would not have you harm yourself physically—that's asceticism. Before attempting extensive fasting, consult your physician.

INTRODUCTION

When I came to work with Jerry Falwell in Lynchburg, Virginia, in 1971, to help start Liberty University, I discovered that Jerry not only made it a personal practice to fast for finances, but he also encouraged and taught his congregation to do so. So when Jerry called for an all-church fast to pray for money for the university, it was second nature to him—but not to me. In fact, I was intimidated by the challenge. As a leader in the newly established school, I found myself wondering, *What will happen if I can't fast successfully?* The truth was, I didn't know how to fast.

That first fast was a one-day Yom Kippur fast, which meant we would go without food from sundown Sunday night to sundown Monday night. Just as the Jews in the Old Testament fasted on the Day of Atonement, or Yom Kippur, from sundown to sundown, so we followed that pattern in Lynchburg.

As the day of the fast drew near, I worried that I would get hungry and eat. Worse yet, I worried that I would get sick. Most of all, I worried about my reputation: *What would people think if I failed?*

I have three fond memories of that particular fast. First, it was not nearly as difficult as I feared. Second, I felt close to God as I fasted. Third, when the financial answer came, I felt very much a part of that answer because I had learned to sacrifice when I prayed. So if you're afraid to try fasting, I understand. My advice is to start small—a one-day fast is perfect. You can work your way up over time to longer fasts.

GETTING OUT OF A FINANCIAL HOLE

When I first moved to Lynchburg, I still owned a house in the Greater Chicago area. After several months of paying two mortgages—the mortgage in Lynchburg was paid on the first of the month, the mortgage in Chicago on the fifteenth—I asked my wife to join me in fasting that God would find a buyer for the house in Chicago. She agreed, and we fasted on the fifteenth day of the month after mailing in our house payment. Nothing happened. I forgot about the fast until the next month when I had to mail in another house payment. Again, my wife and I fasted—and again, nothing happened. We continued this process of fasting for about six months with no visible results.

Then one day the realtor phoned me. "We've got a live prospect on the hook," he announced. But with nothing definitely settled, my wife and I continued our monthly fasts. After about a year of fasting, the house finally sold, and I went to Chicago for the closing. It was then that the buyer told me, "I first looked at your house a year ago on my wife's birthday." As we compared notes, I discovered that his wife's birthday was the day after my wife and I had completed our first day of fasting.

From this experience I learned a few things. First, when we begin fasting and praying, we shouldn't give up. God's answer may not be no; it may be wait. So keep on praying—and keep on fasting. Jesus said there were some situations that could only be handled "by prayer and fasting" (Matt. 17:21). The word "fasting" here indicates continuous action, implying fasting more than once. Second, sometimes prayer is not enough to get what we need from God, so in difficult situations we may need to add fasting to our prayers. My wife and I had been trying to sell a house in a real-estate market where nothing was moving. But God honored our prayer and fasting, and we got out of a financial hole. So if you find yourself facing financial problems, consider praying *and* fasting for a solution.

LEARNING THE NINE FASTS OF ISAIAH

Twenty-five years ago I began teaching the student leaders at Liberty how to fast. I prepared a lesson from Isaiah 58:6-8, which gives nine practical results for people who fast.

> Is this not the fast that I have chosen: to loose the bonds of wickedness, to undo the heavy burdens, to let the oppressed go free, and that you break every yoke? Is it not to share your bread with the hungry, and that you bring to your house the poor who are cast out; when you see the naked, that you cover him, and not hide yourself from your own flesh? Then your light shall break forth like the morning, your healing shall spring forth speedily, and your righteousness shall go before you; the glory of the Lord shall be your rear guard (Isa. 58:6-8).

When I taught the students, I explained how each of the nine results of fasting would influence them.

My nine-part lesson based on the above Scripture passage was as follows:

1. "To loose the bonds of wickedness" was the Disciples' Fast to break addiction and besetting sins.
2. "To undo the heavy burdens" was the Ezra Fast to solve problems.
3. "To let the oppressed go free" was the Samuel Fast for evangelism and revival.
4. To "break every yoke" was the Elijah Fast to break discouragement and burnout.
5. "To share your bread with the hungry" was the Widow's Fast to supply physical necessities for the poor.
6. "Your light shall break forth" was the Saint Paul Fast for insight and decision making.
7. "Your healing shall spring forth speedily" was the Daniel Fast for health and healing.
8. "Your righteousness shall go before you" was the John the Baptist Fast for influence and testimony.
9. "The glory of the LORD shall be your rear guard" was the Esther Fast for spiritual warfare and protection from the evil one.

These nine fasts are explained in more detail in my book *Fasting for Spiritual Breakthrough*. While that book discusses how fasting solves problems in a general way and how to gain new insights by fasting, it does not discuss fasting to solve financial problems. Just as that book gives an overview of fasting in general, the book you are now reading specifically looks at how fasting can help solve money troubles.

And that's the reason I've written this book. I have spent my entire ministry working in struggling Christian colleges, spending a great deal of time raising money. After 50 years of ministry,

I know firsthand that God does answer prayer. He has faithfully supplied the needs we have brought to Him in prayer, and I praise Him for His mercy and for His supernatural intervention in our financial struggles time and again. It has been a thrilling journey—as it will be for you, as you learn to seek His provision through prayer and fasting.

Enjoy the stories, study the principles, and learn about fasting for financial breakthrough.

Sincerely yours in Christ,
Elmer Towns
From my home at the foot of the
Blue Ridge Mountains
Winter 2001-2002

CHAPTER 1

FASTING AND PRAYER FOR FINANCIAL INTERVENTION

I was shocked when I picked up the phone to hear someone say, "You dirty dog!" Not many people greet one another over the phone that way. Although I didn't know the exact identity of the caller, I could tell from the chuckle that accompanied his unusual greeting that it was one of my friends. With a laugh, I demanded, "Who is this? Identify yourself."

"This is your good friend Ron Phillips," the caller answered. "I'm at the Southern Baptist Convention, but I'm not going to the sessions and I'm not in the halls talking to my pastor buddies. I'm stuck in this hotel room reading your book. I just can't put it down." He then told me that God was speaking to him about leading his church into the spiritual discipline of fasting.

ONE CHURCH'S EXPERIENCE OF FASTING

Some time earlier I had sent Ron a typed copy of the manuscript for my book on fasting and asked for his critique. In addition to telling me he couldn't put the manuscript down, he said, "You must come to my church to speak. You messed up my enjoyment of the convention, so now you've got to come teach my people about fasting."

We agreed on a mutually convenient date for the speaking engagement and then he told me, "I'll have 800 people there for an all-day Saturday seminar, because we must learn about fasting." That was a bold claim, since his church averaged 1,200 in attendance, and 800 was a very large percentage of his congregation—but he was so sure the people would respond. As it turned out, his estimate was a bit optimistic. Only 154 members of the Central Baptist Church congregation attended the seminar. We later wondered if we had scared many away by asking them to fast that day for the first time.

Despite the smaller-than-expected turnout, the seminar went well. I taught from 8:00 A.M. to 3:00 P.M. and was ready to close when Ron jumped up to ask everyone present to volunteer to fast and pray one day each month for revival in the church. He even appointed one of the women to be the prayer coordinator. A team of 123 prayer intercessors promised to begin that very day to fast and pray for revival.

When I first got to the church, they had just finished a Sunday-through-Wednesday evangelistic conference. Twelve people came forward for salvation, re-dedication and church membership—not much in results for a three-day conference.

But the church didn't have much spiritual power—yet.

A few months later, the church announced a one-week out-reach event. Because they had fasted and prayed, the power of God was demonstrated and the revival continued for an extra week. Communal fasting and prayer had worked! A total of 998 people made spiritual decisions; worship attendance jumped by 401 that week; Sunday School attendance increased by 257. The offerings that month were $500,000 more than what had been offered the same month in the previous year. Sound incredible? Not when God is involved. *And maybe what God did for them, He will also do for you!*

The church soon took on a new spirituality and prospered. When attendance reached 3,500 weekly, the church faced several decisions. Would they expand the present auditorium or build a new one? If they were to build a new one, what type of auditorium would they build and where on their property would they build it? To answer these and other pressing questions, Pastor Phillips called for a churchwide 40-day fast so that everyone could pray and become part of the decision. But he didn't ask for everyone to fast in the same way. He knew most members couldn't fast completely for 40 days, so he asked the people to fast according to what they felt they were able to do (technically, this is called a partial fast). He suggested these options as examples of different types of fasts:

- Give up one or two meals a day and pray during those mealtimes.
- Give up meat.
- Fast every other day.
- Give up television and spend that time in prayer.
- Give up weekly sports and spend that time in prayer.
- Give up all desserts, snacks and sweets.
- Join the pastoral staff on a 40-day juice fast.

Each person was asked to enter at least one fast at his or her level of availability and understanding. All were fasting for God's guidance regarding the building expansion and revival of the church. At the end of the fast, Pastor Phillips said, "The greatest result of our 40-day fast was not the tangible answers we were seeking. Our greatest result was the spiritual growth of our members. People took steps of faith they had never attempted before. They trusted God at a level we had never experienced."

Can you ask God for big things in the same way as the people of Central Baptist Church did? If your answer is no, it may be that you have a faith problem. Often people have trouble asking God for money or trusting him for "big things," because they simply don't have the faith.

When the disciples were faced with a miracle they couldn't understand, Jesus challenged them with this statement: "Have faith in God. For assuredly, I say to you, whoever says to this mountain, 'Be removed and be cast into the sea,' and does not doubt in his heart, but believes that those things he says will come to pass, he will have whatever he says" (Mark 11:22-23). If we have faith, we can say to our money problem "Be removed," and we will have our answer.

PROPER INGREDIENTS FOR DESIRED RESULTS

When cooking, we have to use the correct ingredients to produce the desired results. When I first met Ruth, she wanted to prepare one of my favorite meals—deviled crab. She had never baked deviled crab—she didn't even like seafood—so she didn't know how delicious deviled-crab casserole tasted. She followed a recipe but made one mistake—only one, but it was a significant one— that ruined the meal. Instead of two teaspoons of mayonnaise, she added two cups! The casserole was terribly greasy and didn't taste at all like deviled crab. But since true love always finds a way, I ate it.

In the same way, God may answer our prayers because we meet *most* of His criteria—but maybe not. Why take the chance? Wouldn't it be better to follow His instructions exactly and be sure of the outcome? When we are wholly (and holy) ready to meet His conditions, we can trust that our prayers will be answered. There are seven ingredients that I believe result in successful prayer and fasting.

SEVEN INGREDIENTS OF PRAYER AND FASTING

1. Fast and pray according to God's will.
2. Fast and pray according to biblical principles.
3. Fast and pray in faith believing.
4. Fast and pray in fellowship with another believer.
5. Fast and pray continuously.
6. Fast and pray to be cleansed of sin barriers.
7. Fast and pray with a great number of people.

Fast and Pray According to God's Will

When we fast and pray for money, we should make sure that we are asking for things that God wants us to have. When I was a small boy, my mother would send me to the convenience store two blocks away to get items for a meal. I didn't need to take money, as the storekeeper had a small charge book with the name "Towns" written across the spine of the book. Whatever items I bought, he listed in that book; then I signed my name. At the end of the week, my mother would settle up the account.

I remember that on one occasion when my mother sent me for some groceries, I told the man behind the counter, "Also, my mother wants a Coca-Cola and a candy bar."

The man squinted his eyes and asked, "You're sure your mother wants a Coca-Cola and a candy bar?"

"Yes, sir," I said. Then, in my naiveté, I added, "She wants it opened."

Halfway home I stopped in an empty field behind a billboard to drink the Coke and eat my candy bar. Obviously, I had lied to the man and I was stealing from my mother. Just as God has a day to execute justice for those who have sinned against Him without repentance, so my mother executed justice on me when I got home. The storeowner had phoned to tell her what I'd done, and although I wouldn't say she hurt me with her spanking, I did feel as if I were being executed.

So what's the point of the story? When you fast and pray, make sure you ask for those things that God sends you to get— *ask according to His will*. The Bible says, "If we ask anything according to His will, He hears us. And if we know that He hears us, whatever we ask, we know that we have the petitions that we have asked of Him" (1 John 5:14-15).

If we ask anything according to His will,
He hears us. And if we know that He hears us,
whatever we ask, we know that we have the
petitions that we have asked of Him.

1 JOHN 5:14-15

How do we know God's will? We find His will in the Scriptures. When we're fasting for money, we first get into the Word and find out what it has to say about the subject. When we know what the Bible says about something, we know God's will in that area. Note the following suggestions about finding God's will:

- Follow the admonitions such as repent, pray, get baptized, live holy and worship God.
- Don't break the obvious laws of God, such as the Ten Commandments—e.g., don't steal, take God's name in vain or commit adultery.
- Don't violate your conscience.
- Work hard at your vocation.
- Serve the Lord according to the gifts, or abilities, He has given you.

Finding and doing God's will is a lifelong journey. We are commanded to know it: "Understand what the will of the Lord is" (Eph. 5:17). Then we are commanded to do it: "Be obedient . . . doing the will of God from the heart" (6:5-6). So the closer our request for money is to the will of God, the more likely we will get a favorable answer. *Is the money that you believe you need God's will for you?*

Fast According to Biblical Principles

When we're fasting, we must set aside time to study and reflect upon the Word of God. In the previous section, we addressed reading the Bible in order to find what God's will is and know how to pray accordingly. This section deals with the method of prayer, or how we should ask. When fasting, we should read longer-than-usual daily portions of Scripture to learn how to pray. But more than reading, we must *study* the Scriptures carefully to understand what God has promised. Also when fasting, we will want to memorize Scriptures that become the basis of our request:

- We ask according to Jesus' name (see John 14:13-14).
- We ask because we abide in Jesus (see John 15:7).
- We ask continually (see 1 Thess. 5:17).

Two things happen as we study God's Word while fasting. First, when we're fasting, we are probably more controlled by the Holy Spirit than at any other time. Therefore, the Holy Spirit, who is our teacher (see John 14:26), will come to explain with greater spiritual insight about how to pray. But there's also a second thing that happens when we fast: Our physical heart and entire digestive system can rest. Rather than our heart working hard to pump blood to the stomach for digestion, it relaxes and more blood flows into our brain. We think more clearly during a fast than at normal times; we can learn more naturally while fasting. Therefore, as we fast and pray, we will learn greater lessons on prayer. Remember Jesus' words, "If you abide in Me, and My words abide in you, you will ask what you desire, and it shall be done for you" (John 15:7).

> If you abide in Me, and My words abide in you, you will ask what you desire, and it shall be done for you.
>
> JOHN 15:7

Sometimes, when I am asking for things that stretch my faith beyond normal expectations, I read again the great passages that magnify our awesome God. Only then, when I begin to understand the awesome power of God, can I ask in faith for a big financial breakthrough.

Fast and Pray in Faith Believing
When the disciples couldn't get their prayers answered, they requested of the Lord, "Increase our faith" (Luke 17:5). Jesus' answer to them indicates what we must do when we ask for more faith: "If you have faith as a mustard seed, you can say to this mulberry tree, 'Be pulled up by the roots and be planted in the sea,' and it would obey you" (v. 6). Do you have faith that

God can solve your money problems?

Jesus explained that the issue was to have faith the size of a mustard seed. This seed is one of the smallest particles in existence, so small you can barely see it with the naked eye. But Jesus was not talking about the size of our faith; He was talking about the necessity of having faith, as opposed to not having it. He said that if we have faith—no matter how little—we can get answers from God. We therefore learn two principles about faith from Jesus' illustration.

First, it is not the *degree* of faith that gets the job done; it's the existence of faith that matters. If we have faith—as opposed to those who don't have it—we can dig up a tree by its roots. How does this relate to financial breakthrough? If we have *any* faith in God, we can fast and pray for money answers.

Second, God often uses what is weak and little to accomplish a gigantic task. Just as the mustard seed is small but does a great task, so our small faith can move heaven. We can use our small faith to fast and pray for God to cast our money barriers into the sea.

PASSAGES TO BUILD YOUR FAITH

Genesis 1

Exodus 14:29-31; 16—17; 19—20; 33:1—34:9

Joshua 3

Psalms 19, 29, 91, 103, 139

Isaiah 6; 37; 40—42

Daniel 4

John 6

Acts 2; 5:1-42

Ephesians 1—3

Revelation 1; 4—5; 19—22

Fast and Pray in Fellowship with Another Believer

There is a principle here that we need to understand: Small doors may open up to large rooms. There is power when two or more pray together. Jesus said, "If two of you agree on earth concerning anything that they ask, it will be done for them by My Father in heaven" (Matt. 18:19). Notice the condition of praying with someone else: Both must agree in prayer. That means each person must get rid of pride and pretense. To agree means to be honest with one another before God. On what should you agree? Agree that the request is God's will. Agree that neither of you has hidden sin. Agree that you both meet the biblical formula for receiving answers to your prayers. Agree that the faith of the other is effective. And agree to keep asking until the answer comes.

Think of Paul and Silas praying in prison at midnight until there was an earthquake (see Acts 16:16-34). Their agreement got an answer. What about Peter and John going into the Temple at the house of prayer (see 3:1-10)? A beggar asked for money, but Peter and John healed him instead. That was agreement. And don't forget Moses' interceding on a hill overlooking Joshua's fight with the Amalekites (see Exod. 17:8-16). While Moses stretched his arms to God, the Israelites won; when Moses became weary and dropped his arms, the battle went against God's people. Two men—Aaron and Hur—stood by to hold up Moses' arms. Those two men helped win the battle. What can you and someone else accomplish?

- Agree that the request is God's will.
- Agree that neither of you have hidden sin.
- Agree that you both meet the biblical formula for answers.
- Agree that the faith of the other is effective.
- Agree to keep asking until the answer comes.

Al Henson graduated from Liberty University in 1978 and began a church in Greater Nashville, Tennessee. When the church was only two months old, Al discovered 25 acres on I-24, not far from the apartment building where he lived. As he drove past and saw a tenement house on the property, he sensed that the site might be purchased. When he first contacted the owner, the man refused to sell the land because he planned to will the property to his daughter. When Al called the owner a second time, he received another no—this time more emphatic than the first. But then, because of the leading of the Lord, Al walked the property line to ask God to give his congregation the tract of land. On several occasions he returned to kneel on the property and ask God to give it to the church.

Finally, Al fasted and prayed for three days that God would touch the owner's heart. He also got the church to pray with him for the property. Then he visited the owner to share his burden for reaching the city of Nashville. As he left, Al asked the man, "Will you pray about selling the property to us?" Before he could answer, the man's wife said, "I'll see that he prays about it."

The next morning, while Al was shaving, the man phoned to tell him he wasn't able to sleep all night. The owner said, "The Lord spoke to me as I have never heard Him speak to me before. I know God wants you to have this property." Then he went on, "If you will come up with $29,000, I will loan you the other $71,000 to buy the property." The property was valued at $175,000. The owner had agreed to give the rest as a gift to Al's church! If God answered the prayers and fasting of Al Henson, He can solve your money problems too.

Fast and Pray Continuously

In the introduction I shared the story of how my wife and I prayed and fasted for one year to sell a house in Chicago. Sometimes God wants us to ask once to get an answer, and so we ask in faith just once, knowing God will respond. At other times, God knows it will take time to get an answer, so He wants us to keep on asking. By faith, we pray for a long time before we get an answer. God's Word tells us, "Men always ought to pray and not lose heart" (Luke 18:1). Paul said, "Pray without ceasing" (1 Thess. 5:17). Have you given up, or are you willing to continue fasting and praying until you get an answer? If you are willing to continue, let me encourage you: Keep on asking the Father, and it will be given to you. Keep on looking for an answer from God, and you will find it. Keep on knocking on the door to heaven, and it will be opened to you (see Matt. 7:7).

WHY DOES GOD WANT YOU TO KEEP ASKING?

• Your answers may take time.
• You need to learn patience.
• You need to learn stewardship.
• You need to change your request.
• An answer may glorify you, not God.
• You need more faith.

Some financial problems cannot be solved in one prayer meeting. We may have to pray through many paychecks and suffer many bill collectors. God may not solve our money problems instantly. God may be telling us that we have something to learn first, but we may not be paying attention. So we have to keep on asking. It's not that God doesn't hear or that He can't answer. It may be that we're just not paying attention. Is it possible that you are the cause of your money problems?

God wants all of His children to be better stewards of their finances. God knows that sometimes the greatest miracle is not the miraculous supply of money—it is when we learn money discipline. To change the way some of us think and act about money can be a greater miracle than a supernatural supply of money. Why? Because some of us are shoddy disciples and therefore an embarrassment to the church family. If God sent poor stewards $100,000 miraculously, that miracle would not glorify Him in the eyes of their creditors, because those creditors consider them a bad risk. Sadly, some Christians can't be trusted to pay their bills on time. But God doesn't tell these bad risks no outright when they ask for money; He tells them to wait. He tells them to wait, pray and learn some lessons. What lesson does God want them to learn? He wants them to learn how to s-t-r-e-t-c-h their money further, how to sacrifice today's pleasures to pay for yesterday's mistakes, how to spend money today in light of future plans. Then one day they'll reestablish their credit and live within their income. God will get greater glory when they learn to handle their money properly than He would if He sent them $100,000.

The problem is that these people are in a dark money hole and they want help now. But the bottom line is not getting money when we want it; the bottom line is glorifying God. So we keep on asking, keep on seeking, keep on knocking. A transformed attitude about money will glorify God more than winning the lottery. And we must remember, there are reasons why God wants us to keep on asking. Our answers may take time, but we need to learn patience. We need to learn stewardship. Perhaps we need to change our request. An immediate answer may glorify us, not God; it takes time to turn that around. We need more faith.

Fast and Pray to Be Cleansed of Sin Barriers

God will not hear and answer our requests when there are sin barriers in our lives. "If I regard iniquity in my heart, the Lord will not hear" (Ps. 66:18). Isaiah said that sin blocks God's hearing: "Behold, the LORD's hand is not shortened, that it cannot save;

nor His ear heavy, that it cannot hear. But your iniquities have separated you from your God; and your sins have hidden His face from you, so that He will not hear" (59:1-2). Even the blind man in Jesus' day realized that sin keeps prayers from being answered: "We know that God does not hear sinners" (John 9:31).

Perhaps we have money problems because of sin. This could be known sin or even unknown sin. Let's discuss known sin first. If we are consciously breaking a commandment, God will not answer. Do we have a bad temper, use bad language or knowingly bounce checks?

We must treat known sin according to the Bible's formula for obtaining forgiveness. First, we confess it to God, which is more than saying "I'm sorry." The Bible tells us, "If we confess our sins, He is faithful and just to forgive us our sins" (1 John 1:9). Confessing is not just saying what we think or even how we feel. Tears are not enough. When we confess to God, we are saying the same thing about our sin that God says about it. And God says that all sin is an abomination.

After confessing our sin to God, we deal with our sin spiritually—we repent, or turn away from the sin, and promise never to do it again. If we wronged or defrauded someone and need to make restitution, we do so. If we need to heal a broken relationship and it is within our ability to do so, we do it. Each time we deal with a past sin, we should learn something more about living in the future. We realize what was lost because of sin and, hopefully, we determine never to do it again. We learn what restoration means and what God would do if we go back to that sin.

Maybe our problem isn't something we're aware of. Maybe our problem is hidden sin, ignorant sin or forgotten sin. Some sins are like germs—hidden from the human eye but still real and dangerous.

A faculty colleague who was violently vomiting and had a high fever was taken to the hospital. The lab work was done, but the cause of his problem was not discovered. It happened a second and third time, but still the lab could not find the source of the problem. The whole family was then seized with similar symptoms. After examining the home, they found a set of teacups that had been purchased abroad. The teacups had been painted with lead paint and not properly sealed in a pottery kiln. As a result of using the cups, they all had suffered from various degrees of lead poisoning.

Undetected and unconfessed sin can affect us like lead poisoning. We can repeatedly become spiritually sick without knowing the cause. What can we do? We can search for hidden sin by fasting and praying until we discover the cause.

- Learn what you lost because of sin.
- Determine to never do it again
- Learn what restoration means.
- Learn what God would do if you go back to that sin.

Fasting is a time when we do more than ask for money. It is a time to reexamine our relationship with God. We search our heart by asking God to examine us and reveal any sin that we can't see. The psalmist prayed, "Examine me, O LORD, and prove me" (Ps. 26:2). Job prayed, "Let me be weighed in a just balance, that God may know my integrity" (Job 31:6). God may not give us a financial answer because we haven't searched deeply enough, we're not serious enough and we haven't lingered long enough in His presence.

If we have a sin problem and can't find it, what's the answer? First, we recognize that the problem is with us, not with God. Notice the description of God: He is "the Father of lights, with whom there is no variation or shadow of turning" (Jas. 1:17). When we come into God's presence, there is no shadow behind us, under our feet or in our pocket. His light surrounds us. If we can't find our sin, the problem is our location—we're not in God's presence.

When fasting, we must find God's presence, abide in it and fellowship with Him. When I was a small kid, the best time to ask Dad for a nickel was when he was in a good mood. When he was arguing with Mother, I stayed out of sight. But when he was sitting on the front porch reading the paper, that was the time to ask. When is the best time to ask our heavenly Father for money? Not when sin is blocking our fellowship with Him. When we are walking in fellowship with God is the time He begins to answer our requests.

Fast and Pray with a Great Number of People

If there is power when two believers pray in agreement, what happens when 100 believers pray? Or 1,000? Or even a greater number than 1,000? James was arrested and beheaded by King Herod (see Acts 12:1-2). Then Peter was arrested and the Church thought the same type of execution awaited him. "But constant prayer was offered to God for him by the church" (v. 5). Obviously, God heard and answered. He sent an angel to deliver Peter. When Peter got out of prison, he went to a certain home. Which one? The one "where many were gathered together praying" (v. 12).

There is value in the volume of prayer.

JOHN ARNOLD, PASTOR, LIBRARY BAPTIST CHURCH
PITTSBURGH, PENNSYLVANIA

SOLUTIONS FOR CHURCH FINANCIAL PROBLEMS

Saint Peter's Lutheran Church in Fort Pierce, Florida, had an experience with prayer and fasting that started in 1992. Prior to that, the church had been having financial problems. The pastor, Rev. Ted Rice, preached messages on stewardship for four weeks. At the end of the fourth message, he asked the people to try tithing—giving 10 percent of their income—for three months. His part of the bargain was to stay in the sanctuary for the next three days to pray and fast for each of those who agreed to tithe. He then prayed for them each morning for the next 87 days. The church's income more than doubled.

Next, the church property was sold in response to fasting and prayer. When a number of people left the church two years later, the church was short of funds. At the council meeting that month, someone suggested cutting something out in order to pay all the bills. Pastor Rice said they were not going to cut anything. Instead, they would pray and fast for 24 hours. The pastor and the church council met in the sanctuary from Friday at 6:00 P.M. until Saturday at 6:00 P.M. to pray and fast in unity for their congregation's needs.

As a result, the church had the best income that July that it had ever had—enough to carry them through the summer months with no problem. The following week a major drugstore chain offered them $1.3 million dollars for their property. The church countered and eventually settled for $1.4 million. This price was an incredible blessing and a generous offer for only 3.5 acres and an old building that needed a lot of work. Now the church owns 18.6 acres near an interstate exit and is planning to build an 18,000-square-foot sanctuary. God is faithful and able to do what He promises.

Prayer and fasting for money solutions is a good idea. But it is a better idea to get someone to pray and fast with us. Whom can we get to pray with us? Why not our family, our Sunday School class or even our entire church? We should be in fellowship with a group of Christians so that we can ask them for prayer support. If God will not turn a deaf ear to one serious saint pouring out his or her heart to Him, what will be His response when many cry out to Him with one voice?

TAKE-AWAY PRINCIPLES

- We must believe that God cares about our problems and that He will do something about them.
- We need to know that God can give us a spiritual breakthrough to our financial needs.
- We follow the same path for getting answers from God regarding our financial needs as we do for getting any prayer answered.
- We must be in fellowship with God to receive money answers from Him.

CHAPTER 2

FASTING TO BUILD
YOUR FAITH

In the fall of 1979, Liberty University was fasting and praying for
$5 million to complete seven new dormitories. Each dormitory
stood three stories tall and had a completed roof. But inside they
were like empty boxes; the exterior brick walls were the only
things finished. Liberty had run out of money, so Jerry Falwell
asked us to fast and pray for $5 million. This was more money
than I had ever prayed for, and it challenged my imagination. I
just couldn't bring myself to pray with integrity, because I simply didn't have the faith to ask for such a large amount.

Following Jerry's request, the faculty and students
marched out of the chapel and gathered around the buildings.
We all knelt in small circles to pray around the incomplete
structures. I didn't know it then, but a TV camera was looking

over my shoulder. The following Sunday I saw and heard myself praying on television, "Lord, You know I don't have faith for $5 million. That's more than I have ever asked before. While I can't ask You for the money, I ask You for faith to believe You for big things."

Have you ever felt like that? You knew you didn't have faith to ask God to do a miracle. You didn't know why, but you knew the faith wasn't there. That's how I felt that day—and that's why I prayed as I did.

On the same television program I also watched Jerry ask God for $5 million. He prayed, "Lord, we need these buildings for another thousand students at Liberty University. These new students will build churches and become missionaries. They'll be young champions who change the world for Christ. Because we need the money, I am asking You for $5 million."

There was confidence in Jerry's voice. It resonated with me and I knew that he was serious. It also must have resonated with God, because within a few weeks the $5 million came in, and the buildings were finished for the next school year.

Praying by Faith or Feelings?

When the disciples were faced with an insurmountable problem, Jesus told them, "Have faith in God" (Mark 11:22). With the proper faith, the disciples could remove barriers to get the work of God moving. Jesus told them, "For assuredly, I say to you, whoever says to this mountain, 'Be removed and be cast into the sea,' and does not doubt in his heart, but believes that those things he says will come to pass, he will have whatever he says" (v. 23). So when we need money, we should learn to fast and pray for it. We need faith to tell our "money mountain" to be removed and cast into the sea. Jesus promised, "Therefore I say to you, whatever things you ask when you pray, believe that you receive them, and you will have them" (v. 24).

However, we will not always get what we petition God for just because we pray for it. It's like starting up our personal computer. We need to type in our name and password, and sometimes several other commands, just to get our computer online. For my computer, I have to activate my virus-protection program, as well as hook up to my network system drive. Then when I have completed the log-on process by giving my computer all the appropriate commands, a musical chord is heard, and I know I'm up and operating.

It is the same way with fasting and prayer. We don't get our prayers answered just because we quit eating and begin asking. We must ask in Jesus' name, which means being in fellowship with Him. We must ask according to the will of God and the Word of God—we can't have one without the other. We must confess all known sin before we ask, and we must harbor no ill will toward any when we want an answer to prayer.

But the biggest step of all is faith. We must ask in faith. Why? "Without faith it is impossible to please Him, for he who comes to God must believe that He is, and that He is a rewarder of those who diligently seek Him" (Heb. 11:6). With faith we can receive anything that God can give—if we honestly believe God will do what He has promised. How much faith do you have?

What is faith? Faith is affirming what God said in His Word. Affirming means we must want what God's Word promises, obey what God's Word commands, act on the conditions of God's Word and know that the promises in God's Word are real. Is that your response to God's Word? If so, you're living by faith. Now you can begin fasting and praying by faith.

But not all who think they have faith truly do have New Testament faith. When I was leading a different Christian college before coming to Liberty, the music director, evangelism director and business manager all came to me for permission to buy a van for our college's traveling team. But the college didn't have the money, and we were in such deep debt that we couldn't borrow any. The directors and manager maintained that the van could transport a musical team to churches, where they could receive offerings to pay for the van and supply some money for the school. I denied their request two or three times until they found a good used van that an individual would sell and finance for the college.

When the three college leaders came to my office and presented the financial package for the used van, I challenged them to kneel around my desk to ask God's wisdom about the purchase. After we all prayed, I felt that moving forward was God's will, so I said, "Go ahead." Was I stepping out on faith? At the time, I thought so.

We purchased the van, but before the odometer clocked a mile, the van caught fire and burned up. Not only were we without a van, but the college also had to continue making payments on it long before the team could bring in offerings to cover those payments. Costly repair parts had to be ordered from Europe because the van had been manufactured in Germany. It took a year before the van was running again, so it was a year before we could use it to raise money to make the payments.

I felt we had prayed in faith and I felt we had been doing the will of God, but circumstances seemed to indicate otherwise. My feelings about faith misled me because our feelings about faith are not the same thing as faith. Our feelings are based on our desires, while faith is based on Scripture. Faith is knowing—not feeling—we will get the answer because our request is based on Scripture.

There are others who have prayed for money but didn't get it. Maybe there were times when you thought you'd prayed with faith, but you didn't get your request or things just didn't turn out the way you'd expected, as happened to me in the case of the van. I don't know why you didn't get your answer as you'd expected, but perhaps your desires got confused with your faith. The Scripture in James offers one possible explanation: "You ask amiss, that you may spend it on your pleasures" (4:3). Sometimes we don't get what we ask because what we're asking is based on our desires and not God's will. That's why when we pray in the will of God, based on the Word of God, we can pray in faith.

FASTING TO INCREASE OUR FAITH

Perhaps our biggest challenge to financial breakthrough is not getting more money but getting more faith. As I mentioned earlier, when we were praying for $5 million to complete seven dormitories at Liberty University, my problem was not the lack of money, but my lack of faith. I needed to pray like the father who brought his son to Jesus for healing: "Lord, I believe; help my unbelief!" (Mark 9:24). So what should we do if we find ourselves unable to pray in faith? First, we confess our unbelief, as did Bartimaeus. Then we ask for faith so that we can pray effectively.

If you're up against a money problem, maybe that's what you need to do—ask for faith. You believe in God and you know He can

---

When you need faith to trust God for big things, fasting is a great way to develop it.

---

do anything. But when it comes to asking Him for money—especially a lot of money—you know in your heart that you won't get the amount you ask for, because you just don't have enough faith. That's where fasting comes in. When you need faith to trust God for big things, fasting is a great way to develop it.

FASTING TO DEVELOP FAITH

Faith is not something we catch, like a disease. We can't become infected with faith by being exposed to people with faith. Faith is more like an ability, which grows through experience, practice, commitment and sacrifice. Look at the ability to run a marathon. No one can run 26 miles just because he or she wants to, just as no one has faith to move mountains just because he or she sincerely want them moved. I've seen people pray for money, but it doesn't come just because they wanted it. It takes more than sincerity to get prayers answered.

We develop our faith in much the same way we develop our ability to run the marathon. It's like building up our muscles and endurance. First, we have to make a mental decision to run the marathon, realizing it will take long, hard practice runs. Then we have to change our diet, take vitamins, give up desserts and sweets and sacrifice time for practice. We'll have to spend hours running to build up our endurance. As the old saying goes: no pain, no gain.

We grow our faith the same way. It begins with a decision. We must decide that Jesus comes first—before work, entertainment or relationships. We build faith when we put Him before everything.

We must discipline our eating and drinking habits for both running a marathon and building faith. Yes, I'm talking about physical food. But I'm also talking about controlling our emotional appetite. We can't grow faith on sexual fantasies, greed, gossip or self-exaltation.

Next let's talk about practice. Just as marathon runners build up their endurance slowly, our faith is strengthened the same way. I don't know of any overnight spiritual giants. Great faith is developed by daily experiences of Bible study, communion, worship and intercession. Just as we must learn to run one mile before we can attempt a marathon, so we must learn to trust God for daily needs before our faith can move God to supply millions of dollars.

Runners must practice in all kinds of weather, so it follows that faith is developed through all kinds of experiences. We grow our faith when we successfully live through the death of a loved one, learn vital lessons teaching a Sunday School class and share the gospel with an unsaved friend. We grow our faith by successfully living through victories and defeats. Because our Christianity must affect every area of our lives, we develop our faith through all we do.

LEARNING WHAT TO DO WHEN FASTING

If we want more faith, what's the first thing we must do to get it? We must ask God for it. When the disciples realized their inadequacies, they prayed to the Lord, "Increase our faith" (Luke 17:5). For many years my prayer requests included a plea for more faith. I daily prayed for more faith; I even fasted for it. Asking for more faith is the starting place: "You do not have because you do not ask" (Jas. 4:2). But we must pray in wisdom, knowing how to ask, when to ask and for what to ask. "If any of you lacks wisdom, let him ask of God" (1:5).

Sometimes we will have faith to ask for a certain request but not for another. It may be that we know certain things are God's will, so we ask with confidence. "Now this is the confidence that we have in Him, that if we ask anything according to His will, He hears us" (1 John 5:14). Perhaps we don't have faith when we're not sure if the request is God's will. *Is that why you don't get answers?*

Think again about marathon runners. They need constant practice to develop long-range endurance. So we need a long-term commitment to build up our faith. While we're asking for money, God may be saying, "Wait." What do we do while we're waiting? We build up our faith by praying for it.

There are several things marathon runners can do to become winners. They can learn the principles of running, read about great runners and study the reports of past races. Just so, there are several things we can do to develop our faith. When we are fasting, we should spend extra time reading and studying the Word. I personally try to read entire books of the Bible, rather than just a few chapters at a time, during a fast. During a 40-day fast, I read the entire New Testament. We should also give time to studying, exhausting a topic by looking it up in Bible dictionaries, encyclopedias and reference books. And, of course, we can't forget devotional reading of the Scriptures, as well as reading biographies of men and women who lived out the Christian faith. Their examples can stimulate and encourage our own faith.

The strength of our faith doesn't come simply from our knowledge of God. Rather, the strength of our faith comes from applying our Bible knowledge to our lives on a regular basis. Let's look again at the definition of "faith." "Faith" means affirming what God has said in His Word. Think about the word "affirming." As I said earlier, "affirming" means that we agree with the Word, act on the Word and implement the Word in our lives. Faith is putting God's Word into action. We haven't exercised our faith until we've applied God's Word to our problem. But, let me quickly add, we must apply it correctly.

Therefore, if we want to get more faith, we must get more of the Word of God into our lives: "Faith comes by hearing, and hearing by the word of God" (Rom. 10:17). When a woman once asked me how she could have more faith, I held out my Bible to

her and said, "You grow your faith by this Book." Then I went on
to tell her that she had to listen to the Bible, read the Bible, study
the Bible, memorize the Bible and meditate on the Scriptures.
When the Bible guides our thinking and desires, then our faith
can overcome our weakness, and we can trust God to answer the
requests we have made of Him through prayer and fasting.

TAKE-AWAY PRINCIPLES

- I need faith to get answers to my money problems.
- I can grow my faith in order to get greater answers to
  my prayers.
- I can grow my faith by asking for it to increase and by
  applying the truths of the Bible to my daily life.

CHAPTER 3

FASTING TO LEARN STEWARDSHIP

A father bought his young son a hamburger and some fries, but the boy wouldn't eat; he just sat and played with his food. Then the father did what many fathers do—he reached over to get a fry. He just wanted a taste.

"No," the boy said. "Those are my fries," and he tried to slap his father's hand. Just as the father was doing something natural, so his son was reacting the way young, untrained, selfish children react.

The father thought to himself, *My son doesn't realize I bought these fries. He doesn't realize I could punish him and never buy him any more fries. He also doesn't realize I could show my love to him and bury him in fries.* The little boy's reaction to his earthly father is similar to our reaction to our heavenly Father when He asks us for an offering or a tithe.

FOUR TRUTHS ABOUT OUR MONEY

1. Our heavenly Father has allowed us to have the money we possess.
2. We must recognize that everything we possess comes from Him.
3. God could give us a little or a lot more than we have.
4. God could take from us some or all that we have.

ALL WE HAVE IS HIS

All our money—in truth, everything we have—comes from God. Nothing is ours, even though most of us act as if it were. Remember, God gives us health, strength and opportunity—and if it were not for His protective hand, we could lose everything. We could even lose our very lives.

God has allowed some of us to be rich—bushels of french fries—while others are extremely poor—only a fry or two each day. The issue is not how to talk God into giving us more. The real issue is how we will glorify God with the fries we already have.

The Bible teaches that we should be good stewards of what God has given us. In the parable of the talents, Jesus spoke of three servants, or stewards, and how they tended their master's money (see Matt. 25:14-30). The master planned to be gone from home for a time, so he gave each steward a bank account to manage while he was gone. The money in each account was to be used by the stewards to maintain the master's businesses. The first servant was given $1 million; the second, $2 million; and the third, $5 million. It was not their personal money; they were to use it for the master and show a good profit when the books were audited.

After two years the master returned to examine the books. The one with $5 million had used it well and had doubled it. The servant with $2 million now had $4 million. But the servant who had been given $1 million had nothing to show for it, because he had hidden his money in a hole in the ground. As a result, his $1 million was taken from him and given to the most effective money manager. What can we learn about money from this parable?

FOUR TRUTHS ABOUT OUR FINANCIAL OBLIGATIONS

1. It's not our money but His.
2. We are expected to manage our money wisely for the Lord.
3. He will take it away if we mismanage it.
4. He will reward us for proper management.

MONEY REPRESENTS LIFE

Though our stewardship involves more than finances, it does include managing money. Remember, our money in some ways represents our life—including our time, talents and paycheck. For putting in our time, we earn money; for using our talents, we earn money. So in this way, our money represents our life. The Bible teaches that we should manage all our time, talents and money for the glory of God. When we give our money to God, we're giving our life to God. And when we give God a tithe—10 percent of our income—we are acknowledging that God owns all our money.

There are times when we have money problems, because we don't recognize that all our money belongs to God. Maybe we're not putting God first with our money. Maybe we've been spending too much on luxuries or things we *think* we need. As a result, we have money problems because we haven't been good money managers. We buy the wrong things—too little, too much—at the wrong time. To become a better money manager, we need to fast and pray. When we fast and pray, God may supernaturally supply our needs. In addition, we may learn some principles of proper money management as we stand before Him in prayer and fasting.

Sometimes we have money problems because we haven't tithed to God. He then withholds His full blessings from our lives, and that hurts us. If the little boy with the fries slaps the father's hand once too often, the father may take away those fries.

When studying God's Word, we may find that there are biblical reasons for our money problems. We may be managing our money contrary to God's standards. If that's the case, we need to repent. And remember, repentance requires a change of mind and heart. We may need to change our mind about the way we spend or manage money. If we don't change our thinking along those lines, we'll probably get into money problems in the future, just as we have in the past. Consider what John Wesley had to say about stewardship in his paraphrase of Luke 16:12:

> None of these temporal things are yours; you are only stewards of them, not proprietors: God is the Proprietor of all; He lodges them in your hands for a season: but they are still His property. Rich men, understand and consider this. If your steward uses any part of your estate (so called in the language of men) any further or any otherwise than you direct, he is a knave: he has neither

conscience nor honour. Neither have you either one or the other, if you use any part of that estate, which is in truth God's, not yours, any otherwise than He directs.[1]

Getting lots of money won't get us out of trouble. Even winning the lottery will not solve our money problems if we don't know how to manage the money we win. If we can't manage a small amount of money, we'll quickly get into trouble if we get a windfall of money. If we're poor stewards, we'll eventually lose whatever money we have. Of course, the more money we have, the longer it may take for us to go through it. Stewardship is the proper management of time, talents and money for the glory of God.

Stewardship is the proper management of time, talent and money for the glory of God.

We Must Learn Biblical Stewardship

An earthly father is to provide for his children's needs, just as the father was providing for his son by buying him a hamburger and some fries. In the same way, our heavenly Father will provide for our needs. But remember, it's our *needs* the Father has promised to provide for—not our desires, nor our luxuries. If we have a swimming pool in our backyard—a luxury—then we thank our Father for it. We may not need it, but if we have one, we can enjoy it—without guilt—to the glory of God. However, I'm not sure that we should fast and pray for a swimming pool, a color television or even an air-conditioned car. But we can definitely fast and pray for necessities.

On the one hand, we're not as likely to get into money problems if we're good managers. But being a good manager requires a day-in and day-out commitment, diligently managing our money from week to week and year to year. But problems come into all of our lives—emergencies we don't expect, such as sickness, layoffs, natural disasters and recessions. Some people live in a repressive economy—even an anti-Christian economy. It is during times like these that we can fast and pray for God's intervention.

But let's look at the other hand. Suppose we're in trouble because of poor management. God could give us a financial miracle, but He probably won't if He knows we would just get back into the same money hole. How does He know that? Because we have not changed the way we handle money. We need to learn how to properly use our money; we need to learn the principles of biblical stewardship. We can learn that type of stewardship by living out four basic principles of fasting.

1. Fast for Self-Control

As we fast, we learn to control our physical appetite. We can also make fasting an opportunity to learn how to control our finances. The good thing about fasting is that we get God's help to discipline our fleshly desires. We can then put our newfound self-control to work to discipline our financial appetite. Here are some points of prayer to consider as we fast to gain self-control:

- We pray for insight into why we can't control our money.
- We pray for wisdom to understand the principles of controlling our money.
- We pray for strength to manage our money—continually.
- We pray for shopping wisdom as we cut up our credit cards.

Perhaps we will need to practice fasting many times to get our financial checkbook in order, and it may take time to get our money thinking in order. So we plan to fast repeatedly. Instead of fasting seven days for a money miracle, we might consider fasting once a week for seven weeks. As we exercise restraint in eating, we will learn something about financial control. But old habits—spending habits—die hard. We may need to fast one day a week for an entire year—that's right, 52 times! That way we'll be reminded once a week to control our money, just like once a week we pay bills.

There's another way to help learn financial control—cut up our credit cards. We put ourselves on a cash-only budget. In other words, if we don't have the money with us, then we don't buy anything. We might have to learn to do without luxuries and maybe even some necessities. (When we consider what it's like to live in some Third World countries, we get a new understanding of what necessities really are.) As we fast, pray and discipline ourselves to manage without credit cards, we'll gain a whole new level of self-control.

2. Fast for Insight About Money

When we fast, we get spiritual insights we've never had before. As we remain in God's presence, the indwelling Holy Spirit is able to speak to us: "The Helper, the Holy Spirit, whom the Father will send in My name, He will teach you all things" (John 14:26). We need to pray specifically for money wisdom.

3. Fast for Analysis

As we pray and fast, we need to ask God why we're in financial trouble. Before we can fix a stalled car engine, we've got to learn the cause of the problem. As the old saying goes, "A problem well-defined is a problem half-solved." It is helpful to list all of the reasons that contribute to our financial difficulties. Then we can rank them in order of seriousness. We can also ask God to help us understand ourselves: "If any of you lacks wisdom, let him ask of God" (Jas. 1:5). Once we have a list of the things that cause our money problems, we can pray daily about each item. We can also study the Scriptures to find out what God says about our specific money problems. In addition, there are many good books that outline biblical stewardship, many of which are listed as recommended reading at the end of this book. As we avail ourselves of all these resources, we are self-counseling our way through our problems.

4. Write During Fasting

Some of the best journaling I've ever done was during a 40-day fast. I suggest that on the days you fast about your money problems, you also begin to write down what you are learning about money management. Create a special page on this topic, and go back and add any additional principles as you discover them.

LIVE ACCORDING TO BIBLICAL PRINCIPLES OF MONEY MANAGEMENT

The following is a list of basic money management truths. As you read, carefully consider each one and ask the Lord to transform your thinking about money so that you have His viewpoint, not your own.

- Biblical money management is not about getting more money from God to spend but managing the money we already have.
- Biblical money management is putting God first, necessities second and pleasures last.
- Biblical money management recognizes that money represents life; it's not just spending power.

- Biblical money management is living and spending money according to specific principles.
- Biblical money management leads to spiritual *and* financial victory.
- Biblical money management involves living by the proper use of our money, not by the accumulation of wealth.
- Biblical money management teaches us that we cannot prosper in the future by foolishly spending money today, ignoring yesterday's lessons.
- Biblical money management teaches us that God will take care of us when we are properly related to Him and we properly give to Him.
- Biblical money management teaches us to find our happiness, satisfaction and contentment in God, not in the things we buy.
- Biblical money management teaches us that small victories in money matters can lead to a prosperous life.

SEE THE VALUE OF TWO-PRAYING AND FASTING

When we really want God to answer our prayers, we need to get someone to fast and pray with us. Jesus pointed out the effectiveness of this type of prayer: "Again I say to you that if two of you agree on earth concerning anything that they ask, it will be done for them by My Father in heaven" (Matt. 18:19). If our family finances are in trouble, perhaps we need to fast and pray with our spouse. If it's a personal problem, we can ask a friend to pray with us about our money problem, specifically praying for us to learn biblical principals of money management.

My wife, Ruth, is the most effective prayer partner I have. One evening in 1953, we had a tuna casserole for dinner—not my favorite, but it was cheap. Back then, a can of tuna cost about a quarter, and noodles were a nickel a package. Our proverbial cupboard was bare.

Ruth and I bowed our heads to thank God for our daily bread. In front of us were a few slices of bread, iced tea and Jell-O salad—a simple meal. God had always taken care of us, and we had enough daily bread for that day. But we had nothing for tomorrow—and it was about three days until the next payday.

I was a senior in college at the time, studying for the ministry. I drove a school bus for $1 per hour—not the best of jobs in 1953, but it was all I could get to fit my schedule. Between studying for classes and working in a church, there was not much time to make money. I brought home about $20 a week. In 1953, I felt my wife shouldn't work, so Ruth was a full-time student.

"Thank You for this food," I prayed over the tuna casserole. I was truly thankful for that day; and I knew that God would take care of tomorrow—though I must admit, I didn't know how. Hesitantly but simply, I told God, "You know our need. We don't have any money."

We don't need to pray long prayers for God to answer. He can hear and respond to the shortest cry for help.

"Give us our daily bread . . . "

No sooner had I said "Amen" than we saw a laundry truck pull into our driveway. We knew immediately who it was because our laundryman was not only a neighbor, but he also served as our landlord and collected rent for the owner of our house.

Ruth went to the front door. "I don't have any dry cleaning today," she told him. Smiling, she added, "And if we gave you dirty clothes, we couldn't pay to have them cleaned."

"Oh, no," he answered. "I didn't come to pick up cleaning." He then explained that he had been going over our rental account the previous night. "I came to bring you money," he said.

"When I was going over the accounts, I realized I never paid you for thawing out the pipes."

There had been a hard freeze just after we had moved into our Minnesota home. The temperature had plunged to 40 degrees below zero, and the bathroom pipes had frozen. I borrowed a blowtorch from the school-bus company to thaw them.

Reaching into his pocket, the man took out $20 and handed it to Ruth. "I should have paid you three months ago," he said.

We put the money next to the tuna casserole and prayed again, "Thank You for our daily bread."

God provided miraculously for us, but He did so by using a job I had done earlier—a job that required me to work all day to thaw those pipes. God's timing is always perfect. Three months earlier I had done what I had to do when we needed water. Now, in our hour of need, God reminded the laundryman about the $20 he owed us.

WHAT TWO-PRAY AND FASTING WILL DO FOR YOU

- Make you set realistic prayer goals
- Make you outwardly accountable
- Encourage you to not give up
- Make you more honest in prayer

When we agonize in prayer with a partner and then get an answer, we have someone to rejoice with us. Wouldn't life be empty if we climbed a mountain that we didn't think we could climb, only to get to the top and find we had no one to celebrate with us?

TAKE-AWAY PRINCIPLES

- All our money comes from God.
- God expects us to manage our money for His purposes.
- God will take away our money if we mismanage it.
- God will reward us when we manage our money properly.
- The reason we don't have an abundance of money may be because God can't trust us with it.
- When we take control of our physical appetite, we can also learn to take control of our financial appetite.
- Fasting and prayer are opportunities to learn to manage our time, talents and money for the glory of God.

Note

1. John Wesley, "John Wesley's Notes on the Bible," *Christian Classics Ethereal Library*, October 1, 1997. http://biblestudy.churches.net/CCEL/INDEX.HTM (accessed February 11, 2002).

CHAPTER 4

WHY WE HAVE MONEY PROBLEMS

John and Sue are three months behind on payments on their SUV. They'll have it repossessed if they don't get money soon; if that happens, he'll have to go to work in her car. Will God hear and answer if they fast and pray for car payments?

Frank lost his job a year ago; his unemployment benefits ran out and now he can't make ends meet on welfare benefits. He stands at the four-way stop with a sign "Will work for food." Will God hear and honor his prayers for a job?

A single mom can't meet her rent payment, but she smokes three packs of cigarettes a day and lives on snacks from the convenience store. Will prayer and fasting make a difference?

Almost all of us, at some point or another, have come to the end of a month with more bills than money in our bank account.

This is true not only for individuals but also for religious organizations. Some churches want to build a gymnasium or other building, but they don't have the money. Some missionaries visiting our churches need money for a printing press, a vehicle, a hospital or their personal needs. Almost every work of God needs funding for one reason or another.

There are no easy answers to these problems. It may take a trained money manager to help these people discover if they are wasting money in some way and to teach them how to live within a budget. It may take a supernatural answer to prayer to help others. In any case, people—maybe you—need to determine the reasons for the money problems.

WRONG ATTITUDES ABOUT MONEY

For some people, money burns a hole in their pockets—they spend it as soon as they get it. Maybe they didn't have much money when they were young, so now they react to their meager upbringing and splurge unnecessarily. They're living out a subconscious yearning to spend money.

Others have the opposite problem. They always had money when they were small, and their parents bought them everything they wanted. Spending is not only a bad habit for them—it also has become a destructive way of life. These people have to learn to break their spending habits if they are ever going to get control of their checkbooks. And though it isn't easy, it can be done. Philippians 4:13 tells us, "I can do all things through Christ who strengthens me."

Still others appear to have a money problem, but it's really not about money; rather, it's a discipline problem. They have a problem because they don't know how to wisely use the money they already have.

UNDISCIPLINED DESIRES

Some people buy too much because they have confused needs with wants. They have convinced themselves that they need the things they see advertised on television or in the papers. They think they must have what others have. As a result, they are in debt. These people don't need to fast for a miracle supply of money. They need to fast for reasons related to self-denial. When fasting, we do without food. If we can learn to get along without food, we can learn to get along without other things that may or may not be necessities. Fasting is the beginning of learning how to get along without things for the sake of God.

> When we learn to control our appetite by fasting, we learn to control other areas of our lives.

Perhaps our money problems have nothing to do with our childhood—whether we had too much or too little. We may have money problems because we just can't tell the difference between what we want and what is absolutely necessary—in other words, we are unable to distinguish between needs and wants. Fasting can make a difference. God can teach us the difference between necessities and desires. Fasting can also teach us about life and how to live as a disciple, or disciplined one. *Pray and ask God to teach you how to live a disciplined life.*

ABSENCE OF LONG-RANGE PLANS

Some live from paycheck to paycheck. They don't have any life insurance or retirement fund; there's no such thing as long-range or short-range goals. They simply spend as much as they get. I remember a family man in my church telling me that when he cashed his check on Friday night, he went to the bars to have a good time. On Saturday, he and the family walked through the mall buying what they wanted. They then bought groceries, paid a few bills and took the family out for a big meal. Then he ate peanut-butter sandwiches for the remainder of the week and began the cycle again the next Friday. When he was converted, he told me there was no money for tithing. However, after I taught on stewardship, he realized that God's tithe came first. Putting God first forced him to prioritize his finances. After some time, his clothing got better and he purchased a better house. It's a principle I call Redemption and Lift. When people get saved, every area of their lives improves. They don't waste money on fleshly entertainment or trivial things. With an eternal perception, they discipline their spending, as a disciple of Christ should. *Could this be something God is calling you to do?*

SIN IN OUR LIVES

Some Christians have money problems because of sin. They may be feeding an expensive habit or addiction. Others might spend money on some hidden sin, perhaps even an illicit affair. When we have money problems because of sin, we must begin our fast with repentance. However, if we are unaware of any sin in our lives, then we must fast in order to search our heart for any sins we may have committed in ignorance (see Ps. 139:23-24).

FAILURE TO ASK FOR GOD'S HELP

Some people have money problems because they've gone their own messy way without consulting God's Word regarding financial matters. And still others have never sought God in prayer to ask His help with their financial difficulties. "You do not have because you do not ask," James tells us (4:2). So we must place our financial problems at the top of our prayer list, and then we should begin fasting and praying about them.

GREED

Some people have money problems because they don't have the wisdom, intelligence, training or education to make good financial decisions. Others, however, are simply undisciplined—or lazy. And what about those who lust for money? Some people have a greed problem—that's an entirely different matter. Greed is an addiction, and to break that addiction takes a special fast: the Apostles' Fast. "The love of money is a root of all kinds of evil" (1 Tim. 6:10).

APOSTLES' FAST

1. Fast and pray to renounce any previous or past involvement with satanic practices or false religions.
2. Fast and pray to acknowledge self-deception.
3. Fast and pray to forgive others to get freedom from bitterness.
4. Fast and pray for God's help to learn biblical submission.
5. Fast and pray to get God's help in overcoming pride.
6. Fast and pray to take responsibility for sin in your life.
7. Fast and pray to renounce any sinful influences from family and friends.[1]

POOR MANAGEMENT

Lack of money is not the reason most people are in debt. It's not that they don't have money; it's that they don't know how to manage the money they have. Very few people have more money than they can spend. So what am I saying? Suddenly getting more money won't solve our money problems. After we get a reprieve and perhaps get out of debt, we are soon back in debt because we didn't solve the problem that got us into debt in the first place.

Steve Forbes attended my church in 1996 when he was running for president of the United States. At a special luncheon he attended, I was asked to tell some stories about my poor childhood. Steve later compared my childhood to his. I was extremely poor, and he was extremely rich, but we both had to work for the money we spent. We both valued money because we worked for it.

Even though Steve Forbes owned *Forbes* magazine and was worth over $400 million, he had his daughters work at a McDonald's to learn the value of money. Obviously he had enough money to buy several McDonald's restaurants and give his daughters everything they wanted. Instead, he chose to lead his daughters down a wise path. Maybe learning the value of money is the path you need to take.

Have you ever wondered why God allows some people to make millions but not others? Some Christians are millionaires, while other Christians seem to stay broke. Why is that? Maybe God keeps some believers on a short financial leash because He can't trust them. If they had more money, they'd be skiing in Colorado every weekend, rather than attending and serving in a church. Maybe they'd be on a beach in the Caribbean, paying no attention to God. They might never be in church, never teach Sunday School and never cry tears for the lost. Perhaps the only way God can keep some Christians close to Himself is to keep them poor.

NO FAULT

Some have financial problems through no fault of their own. They may be living during a depression when there are only low-paying jobs—or even no jobs—available. Others live in a section of America or abroad where there are few jobs to be had, even during prosperous times. There is little food and few, if any, options. They want jobs, and they are willing to work hard, but they are locked into poverty because of circumstances beyond their control. To the best of our ability, we should offer assistance and encouragement to such people.

THE VOW OF POVERTY

Historically, many members of the clergy have taken a vow of poverty, which means they will not accumulate wealth or possessions. There are some religious groups that still follow this example. They depend on their church to provide their basic needs. However, most Christian servants receive a salary or stipend. And some have modest possessions and a retirement fund. But they receive marginal salaries and will always have money problems. They trust God to supply their needs.

TAKE-AWAY PRINCIPLES

- Financial problems may be a reflection of a lack of spiritual growth due to disobedience to God.
- Fasting may give us insight into the spiritual and financial reasons for money problems.
- Learning to become disciplined in our finances can lead to becoming a dedicated disciple of Jesus Christ.
- Continual fasting may be necessary to properly deal with greed.

Note
1. Neil Anderson, *The Bondage Breaker* (Eugene, OR: Harvest House, 1990), n.p; and *Freedom from Addiction* (Ventura, CA: Regal Books, 1996), pp. 297-334.

CHAPTER 5

GOD'S SUPPLY FOR CHRISTIAN WORKERS AND INSTITUTIONS

Many believers are in financial straits and it's not their fault. They have followed God's leading for their lives, and they still end up needing money. This includes Christian workers such as church planters, missionaries and evangelists. We've all heard the appeals on radio and television for financial support for various ministries. These appeals have also come in the form of letters. We've even seen appeals from secular charities such as the Red Cross and the United Way. While we don't normally spend a great amount of time or energy praying for secular organizations, what should be our response to appeals from individual Christians and Christian institutions?

EXPERIENCING GOD'S PROVISION FIRSTHAND

I knew beyond a shadow of doubt in 1950 that God wanted me to go to Columbia Bible College (CBC), but my parents couldn't afford to help me pay for it. I had saved $255 from my paper-route money, almost enough to pay the $365 I needed for my first semester of room, board and tuition. Knowing what God had called me to do, I enrolled in college, wondering how long I would be able to stay there. I washed dishes in the "dish pit" for 20 cents an hour, and I washed chandeliers in a chandelier shop for 50 cents an hour. I figured if I put everything I made at both jobs toward my school bill and didn't spend a dime on anything else, I could finish the first semester. I never bought a cold drink or got a haircut (until the dean instructed me to get it clipped short), nor did I wash my clothes in a washing machine. I used the sink in the bathroom.

At the same time, I banged on the windows of heaven daily, begging for money so that I could get through Bible college. I knew that God wanted me in ministry, and I knew God wanted me at that particular college, so I constantly reminded Him that I needed a miracle.

The miracle came, but not in the form of one big check; instead, there were a lot of $5 and $10 checks. When I first got to Bible college, I had written to all my aunts and uncles to tell them God had called me into ministry. I included the gospel in each letter and asked them to accept Christ as their Savior. I don't remember any of them getting saved, but most of them responded like my Uncle Herman, who said to his wife, "Let's send Elmer $10. He's going to be a preacher." My mother came from a family of 11 children and my father from a family of nine. As a result, I received a lot of small checks to finish paying for my first semester, and then I began depositing the extra checks toward the second semester.

In addition, the junior Sunday School class at Bonna Belle Presbyterian Church outside Savannah, Georgia, took me on as their missionary project. They went out into the salt creeks around their homes to catch crabs and steamed them in a giant washtub in the backyard. Then they went door-to-door, selling cooked crabs for a nickel apiece by saying, "Buy a crab and help us put a preacher through college."

When I got a $25 check from these little ones, I locked my dorm room and spread the letter and check out on the bed with gratefulness to God for His provision. Don't tell me God doesn't answer money prayers! I wept in appreciation, promising God that I'd study hard, work hard and make whatever sacrifices were necessary. "I'll not give up," I vowed.

At the end of the first year, I walked away from CBC, carrying everything I owned in a cardboard suitcase, convinced that God could answer prayer in mighty ways. I had personally experienced the truth of Psalm 23:1: "The LORD is my shepherd; I shall not want."

That summer I worked in a shipyard where Navy ships were built. I earned $1 an hour and saved everything I could for the second year of college. I continued banging on the window of heaven for money to continue my education. I believe an angel heard my persistent knocking and asked the Lord to do something. He did! God touched Al Aldridge, a businessman who taught the men's Bible class at Independent Presbyterian Church in Savannah, Georgia, and spoke to his heart. At Al's instigation, the men took a weekly offering to pay the rest of my way through Columbia Bible College.

When we're faithfully doing the work of God and can't look after our own financial needs, He'll look after us. But we have to meet His qualifications. God doesn't waste allowances on lazy or rebellious children.

Many foreign missionaries have chosen a ministry where they will never have a lot of money. They live on meager wages, and they serve in foreign cultures with no luxuries. Most have just enough money to take care of their needs. Even if they work harder, no extra money comes in—longer hours don't mean extra income. When missionaries need money for a new ministry, they must ask for divine intervention. When they need a printing press, a radio tower or a replacement airplane for the one that crashed, they must bang on the window of heaven for a miracle. When they have a medical emergency, what can they do? They cry out to God for a financial miracle. When missionaries need money, the closer they get to the perfect will of God—and the more likely God is to supply their needs miraculously.

THE MODESTO MANIFESTO

1. Honesty in reporting results
2. Financial integrity
3. Sexual purity
4. Unity in the Body of Christ

LEARNING THE MODESTO MANIFESTO: WHY GOD USED BILLY GRAHAM

In the late 1940s, four young men—Billy Graham, Cliff Barrows, George Beverly Shea and Grady Wilson—whom we know today as the leaders of the Billy Graham evangelistic team, met on a farm outside Modesto, California, to pray and seek God's will for their lives and ministries. The farm belonged to the family of Cliff Barrows, the group's music leader. The four men had come to the San Fernando Valley to hold an evangelistic tent crusade. Cliff's father was one of the Christian businessmen who invited the team to Modesto. On the second day, as the team fasted and prayed for God's direction, Billy Graham, the group's leader, directed each man to go off alone to pray for his future ministry. Because they all wanted to be used of God, Billy told them, "I want you to spend an hour thinking about the greatest problems facing evangelistic teams and how we can overcome these barriers."

They made a composite list when they came back together, focusing on four major problems facing them in ministry. These four items are the basis of what became known as the Modesto Manifesto. At the end of the day, each pledged himself to a greater degree of integrity than was found in other evangelistic ministries, promising to support, serve and be accountable to one another. Then they all signed the manifesto.

The first thing on their list was the common misuse of the truth by evangelists. There was a common perception that evangelists exaggerated the size of crowds, the number of converts and the need for money. Each of the young men pledged himself to report the true statistics in their crusades. They were well aware of the accusation of "speaking evangelistically"—a popular statement used as a cover-up when evangelists bragged about their results.

The second concern on their list was money. Because evangelists were always raising money to pay for their expenses, it appeared many were in it for the money. Evangelists also were famous for their appeals for a "love offering." The young team decided to do several things. First, their financial books would always be open. Second, the local committee that invited them for a meeting would vote on a budget and raise the money before they arrived on the scene. This way the control of money was with the committee, not the evangelist. Third, the team eventually began receiving a salary; they did not take a love offering.

The third problem that plagued evangelists was the sexual/moral issue. The group members agreed that they would never ride in a car alone with a member of the opposite sex, nor would they be in a room behind a closed door with a woman. They determined to stay as far from the appearance of evil as possible.

John Corts, president of the Billy Graham Evangelistic Association, used a teaspoon on a dining table to illustrate why they were so careful. He placed the spoon on the edge of the table. As he reached over the spoon for a coffee cup, he eventually knocked the spoon to the floor. He explained, "When an evangelist gets too familiar with women—the spoon on the edge of the table—it inevitably falls to the floor." He then asked, "How can you solve the problem?" He demonstrated the answer to his question by placing the teaspoon as close to the very center of the table as possible. In like manner, Billy Graham and the team pledged themselves that day to stay far away from anything that would even raise suspicion of sexual misconduct.

The four men agreed that the fourth problem of evangelists was a critical spirit. Some evangelists criticized the Church, some criticized other evangelists, and some criticized Christian organizations. The four young men committed themselves to a positive ministry of promoting unity in the Body of Christ.

Although it cannot be denied that the blessing of God is the primary reason for the great success of the Billy Graham evangelistic organization, the Modesto Manifesto is one of the key foundations for the outstanding achievement of Billy Graham and his team. The team covenanted with each other to keep these four principles and to confront one another at the first evidence of a violation of their oath. By holding one another accountable, they silenced the usual criticism about evangelists. They became blameless before the world, reputable to one another and a testimony to God. But more than their covenant-ed protection of each other, Cliff Barrows testified, "We made a commitment to serve and support one another."

LIVING BY MIRACLES

As I said earlier, I am a cofounder with Jerry Falwell of Liberty University. Jerry is the primary spiritual leader, while I am the academic leader. We both pushed continually for more students, more faculty, more buildings and more money. I learned to pray continually for money. Like climbing a mountain, every step up was difficult and threatening. Sometimes it seemed that we hung on to a root or a clump of grass, and there was always the danger of snakes or rockslides. Living by miracles can be dangerous.

Liberty University began small. Jerry would drive his Buick out to nearby country churches in Central Virginia to preach. Doug Oldham, the gospel singer, attracted the crowd with his concerts. I shared the vision of the great university we planned to build that would change the world. Jerry preached, and then at the end he asked everyone to be a "doorkeeper" for Liberty University by giving $1 each week to help support a young "champion for Christ." Everyone who promised to mail $1 each week was given a pack of 52 prepaid envelopes with the reminder to mail $1 each week. Over the years, many have told me that they first began supporting Liberty University when they began sending that weekly dollar. Our faithfulness with the $1 gifts eventually opened the door to millions of dollars in answer to prayer.

But there were financially dark days as well. After the Jim Bakker and Jimmy Swaggart scandals, people stopped mailing money to all TV preachers—Billy Graham and Jerry Falwell included. The university family prayed, but sometimes the needed money didn't come in. Twice I missed a paycheck. When things got tighter, all university executives took a 10 percent pay cut. When the secular labor force was demanding and getting pay raises, faculty at Liberty got only one pay raise in 10 years. Sometimes sacrifice is needed instead of a miracle.

At the time, Liberty was the fastest-growing Christian school in the world. Each year over $27 million in gifts were needed over and above tuition, room and board payments to continue its ministry. But in the mid-1980s, Jim Bakker's and Jimmy Swaggart's falls drew such media attention that it soon became clear that Liberty could no longer raise money through television appeals or by direct mail. Financial giving declined substantially in our ministry, as well as other ministries. Contributions to the Old Time Gospel Hour and Liberty University dropped by about $25 million a year. The university had constructed buildings and had spent about $250 million on facilities, but suddenly we found ourselves unable to raise money to pay our bills. After four consecutive years of $25 million deficits, the university suddenly had approximately $100 million in liability debt. Students were on campus; we couldn't send them home. We had to do something.

Besides the financial debt, Liberty University was threatened with losing its regional accreditation. Because the Southern Association of Colleges and Schools would not renew accreditation for a university that had such huge debts, Liberty had to decrease its debt ratio before it could regain its accredited status. SACS (Southern Association of Colleges and Schools) put Liberty on probation in December of 1996. Without accreditation, we didn't think the university could continue because students wouldn't attend an unaccredited institution. Faced with this crisis, Jerry Falwell fasted seriously.

The Lord had impressed upon his heart in the summer of 1996 that it was time to do what he thought was unthinkable—

to personally go on a 40-day fast. But God had spoken, so he fasted 40 days—July 20 through September 1. As a result, Jerry saw mighty things begin to happen. In that first fast of 40 days, he kept asking God for money. But God impressed upon his heart that he needed to get closer to Him, to listen to Him and to trust Him. When Jerry asked for money, God told him, "Don't look for My pocketbook; look for My heart." Jerry had several lessons to learn before he could ask for money. As he ended that first 40-day fast, he felt he had learned what God wanted to teach him. But he still didn't have an answer about money.

After eating for 25 days, God told Jerry one morning that he could now ask for money. Immediately, Jerry went right back on another 40-day fast that began September 25, 1996, and ended on November 4. He broke the fast that evening.

The first result was that Liberty University received a cash gift large enough to pay off our long-term mortgage debt. Second, the cash flow of Liberty University was replenished with several million dollars, which brought financial and institutional health. Third, God sent Liberty a new president, Dr. John Borek, who had a Ph.D. in business administration and who had been the chief financial officer at Georgia State University. Without him, the university might not have been prepared for SACS's accreditation visit. Fourth, when SACS visited to evaluate Liberty, they removed all sanctions and recommended that Liberty University be reaccredited for 10 years, which was the bottom line of why Jerry had fasted. One individual has given Liberty University close to $50 million since those two fasts.

WRITING A CONTRACT WITH GOD

Bill Bright knew God was leading him to found Campus Crusade for Christ International in the early 1950s. Although he had been a successful businessman, he wanted to make sure his ministry maintained a spiritual focus and foundation. Bill and his wife, Vonette, drew up a contract with God, just as Bill had done when establishing several businesses. But this time it was not a 50-50 contract, as it had been in the secular field. Bill and Vonette gave *all* their money and possessions to God. Bill and Vonette now live in a house and drive a car owned by Campus Crusade. They take no salary and trust God to supply all their personal needs as well as those of Campus Crusade.

Bill has raised millions upon millions of dollars for the *JESUS* film, evangelistic projects and buildings—and the list goes on. God has honored his stewardship of money. Campus Crusade has over 25,000 full-time workers and a volunteer staff of approximately 250,000. It's amazing what money can be raised in partnership with God when He gets all the control and all the glory.

TAKE-AWAY PRINCIPLES

- Some have chosen a vocation in which they will always need to pray for money.
- God is glorified by supplying money for worthy persons and projects.
- Great things can be accomplished for God when He controls the money and gets the glory.

CHAPTER 6

A Faith Approach to Fasting for Money

Kyle and Suzanne were a young couple who were overwhelmed with the usual financial problems that often sink young marrieds—trying to pay off credit-card debt, getting a home started and learning how to live with each other's spending habits. As they fasted and prayed to get their finances in order, God told them to tithe 10 percent, when up to that point they had only been tithing around 3 percent. But their budget told them they would go $400 a month in the hole if they did tithe 10 percent. They continued to fast and pray for help. Then they took the financial plunge and declared, "We will obey God, and we will tithe what God requires." The day after their decision, a friend approached them about moving into an apartment attached to her home. The rent would be $400 per month—$400 less per month than they'd been paying. Once they decided to obey God and tithe, God had immediately provided them with the extra $400 a month they needed to do so.

FAITH-BASED FORMULA

Is there a faith approach that will help our prayers about money get answered? Some naively think all they have to do is ask. While asking is one of God's requirements in prayer, and especially a requirement in prayer about money, asking is not the only step. A lot of things in life require knowing the correct formula. As I said earlier, you can't get into my computer without knowing my name and password. Half of my password is not enough. You've got to get it all correct—down to the last letter—to get into my computer. Also, you can't use my phone for a long-distance call without my code, nor can you get cash with my ATM card or use the copier in my office without the proper personal identification number. So it is with receiving answers for prayer. God wants us to ask *in faith*. Our relationship with God is based on faith, because it is faith—not formula—that pleases God: "Without faith it is impossible to please Him, for he who comes to God must believe" (Heb. 11:6).

Most people don't fast about money until they get into financial trouble; then they cry out to God for help. God often gets our attention through money problems. And from our deepest fears, God conforms our life. As we stay in His presence, *we conform our desires to His will*. There are three points about fasting that help mold us into devoted disciples of Jesus Christ.

FAITH APPROACH TO ASKING

1. Fast to be assured of God's will.
2. Fast to sense God's presence.
3. Fast and study the Scriptures to know God's principles about money.
4. Fast to get insight to how God provides for our needs.
5. Fast to learn priority in money spending.
6. Write a money management plan for life and ministry.
7. Fast to get help in making difficult decisions.
8. Fast to crucify undisciplined money spending.

Fast to Be Assured of God's Will

Before we ask for money, we need to pray and ask God if the problem is an earthly or a heavenly one. Why are we in a dark hole? Before we pray to get out, we need to find out why we're there.

We also need to look for God in our dark valley; *Though I walk through the dark valley of financial death, you are with me* (see Ps. 23:4). Somewhere in our money hole we'll find God. He didn't put us in our hole, but He's there with us. If we look with the eyes of faith, we will see His promise in the dark shadows—*I am with you*. We need to act on that promise and claim His presence. We may be so blinded by fear—job layoffs, overdrawn checkbooks, credit-card debt and maybe even bankruptcy[1]—that we can't see Him in the midst of it. In fact, we may not be looking for Him because we are too busy looking at the challenges confronting us. But He's there. So before we look for money, we must look for God: "Seek the LORD while He may be found, call upon Him while He is near" (Isa. 55:6).

So how do we find God? "You will seek Me and find Me, when you search for Me with all your heart" (Jer. 29:13). When we deprive ourselves of food, we're getting desperate. That tells God we're sincere. He reveals Himself to those who desperately search for Him. When was the last time we used the word "please" when praying? When is the last time we shed a tear before God?

When we fast, we will know God's will—including God's financial plan for our lives—better than at any other time. Why? Because we are closer to God when we fast and we think more clearly when we fast. We see our lives through heaven's perspective, and the Spirit can lead us into truth (see John 14:26; 16:13-15).

Fast to Sense God's Presence

When we deny our physical appetite in order to seek God's presence, He reveals Himself to us. If we want the presence of Jesus in our lives, then we must fast to get it. Just as we can feel the misty rain, so we can feel His presence. Obviously we won't see Him with our physical eyes or touch Him with our fingers, but we will sense His presence in our heart.

Fast and Study the Scriptures to Know God's Principles About Money

When we fast, we must take time to examine what the Bible says about money. Read and study the Scriptures listed to the right:

GOD'S PRINCIPLES ABOUT MONEY

Exodus 20:24; 36:3-7

Exodus 35:4-5,10,30-35

1 Kings 4:7, 27-28 (King Solomon supplied)

1 Kings 10:1-10 (Queen of Sheba)

1 Kings 17:1-7

1 Kings 17:8-16

2 Kings 12:4-8

2 Kings 12:9-16

1 Chronicles 28:12,19

1 Chronicles 29:2-9

2 Chronicles 31:3

2 Chronicles 31:4-10

2 Chronicles 31:11-21

Ezra 2:68-69

Ezra 6:3-15

Ezra 7:6-23

Nehemiah 1:4-11

Nehemiah 2:1-8

Nehemiah 2:11-18

Nehemiah 3; 4:14-21; 6:15

Haggai 1

Matthew 25:14-30

Luke 6:27-38

Luke 8:2-3

Luke 19:11-27

Acts 4:34; 5:2-11

1 Corinthians 16:1-3

2 Corinthians 8–9

TWELVE PRINCIPLES OF STEWARDSHIP

When we understand what God says about money, we'll give it the same value as He does. The following list of 12 principles is only the first lesson in our endeavor to better understand God's economic principles:

1. Stewards recognize that God is the owner of all things and that His followers are stewards who are given the responsibility to manage His resources.
2. Stewards have the freedom and obligation to use their talents, resources and circumstances to get the best results for God.
3. Stewards understand that God does not force His great purpose on the world. God accomplishes His purposes through people.
4. Stewards acknowledge the lordship of Christ over their finances.
5. Stewards who manage money correctly are building biblical character traits within themselves.
6. Stewards are forward thinking in planning their lives.
7. Stewards worship through giving.
8. Stewards are mission minded.
9. Stewards who properly manage their money challenge others to do the same.
10. Stewards must be both students and teachers of God's Word.
11. Stewards understand that God sees their work and will reward them accordingly.
12. Stewards know that their real payday doesn't come at the end of the job; it comes when they stand before God in heaven.

Fast to Get Insight to How God Provides for Our Needs

Many Christians make a habit of praying what I call mailbox prayers. They are always asking God to solve their financial problems with a miracle such as receiving an unexpected check in the mail. Other Christians have more of a lottery mentality when it comes to prayer and think, *Someone's going to win. Why not me?* They want something for nothing. They are sitting around waiting for their ship to come in or for a rich uncle to die and make them wealthy.

But notice how few people in the Bible were delivered from financial problems by a miracle. Most of Israel got their money by working hard on their farms. It was the tithe from their farms that kept the work of God going. Sure, God used the ravens to feed Elijah at the brook (see 1 Kings 17:1-7), and God fed Israel in the desert with manna from the skies for 40 years (see Exod. 16). But millions of believers written about in the Scriptures worked for their food and money. They thanked God for strength to work their land and for the rain and sun that caused their crops to grow. Why should we think that God would work a miracle for us today when He didn't do it for most believers in the Bible? If we think we are an exception, we should be prepared to prove it.

Fast to Learn How to Prioritize Expenditures

Obviously some bills are more important than others. But suppose we have more bills than money. Then we fast and pray to find out where to cut back. But what happens if we think *all* of our necessities are, in fact, real necessities? Now we have a problem. So we fast and pray to determine what necessities are more necessary than others and what necessities have to go. Two cars in the family garage may not be a necessity, especially if public transportation is available. We pray about each item on the list as we try to evaluate them in light of the wisdom God has given us.

Write a Money-Management Plan for Life and Ministry

A money-management plan should include both expected income and expenditures. When we have a realistic view of our income, we can determine which expenses are necessary and how much we can spend on incidentals, luxuries and entertainment. The priorities of our money-spending plan should look something like this:

EXPENSE PRIORITIES

1. Tithes and offerings
2. Housing and utilities
3. Food
4. Clothing
5. Transportation
6. Insurance
7. Education and improvement
8. Retirement
9. Recreation
10. Entertainment

FAST TO GET HELP IN MAKING DIFFICULT DECISIONS

If we are continually in debt, then something is wrong. We need to ask ourselves the following questions:

- Should I take a second job?
- Should my wife/husband work?
- Should I move to a less-expensive home?
- What can I sell?
- Should I cut back in insurance premiums temporarily?
- Should I stop retirement-fund payments temporarily?
- Who, if anyone, in my family can help me financially?
- What money reserve can I use (life insurance, retirement, stocks, etc.)?

Fast to Crucify Undisciplined Spending

Many people have an addiction to spending money. While Paul did not say that he had a money problem, notice his description of himself: "The good that I will to do, I do not do; but the evil I will not to do, that I practice" (Rom. 7:19). We could apply Paul's words to someone with a money problem: Disciplining my money is a good thing, but I don't do it. Spending money on nonessentials is a bad thing, but that's what I do. The problem with addiction is that we go back to it again and again and again. When Paul was faced with his chronic problem, he cried out, "O wretched man that I am! Who will deliver me?" (Rom. 7:24). People who are greedy or have an addiction to spending money seem always to get themselves in a financial hole.

The answer to this sort of money problem comes by putting our lust to death. Paul described it theologically: "Reckon [consider] yourselves to be dead indeed to sin" (6:11). If we are dead, then we won't desire to do anything, have anything or spend anything. What have you ever put to death at the Cross?

Think of a corpse in a hearse being driven from a church to a graveyard. When the hearse drives by the mall, the corpse doesn't want to go buy anything. The corpse has no desire to attend the movies, go into the bar or even go into the fast-food restaurant to get a quick hamburger and milk shake. The corpse has no feelings and no desires. If we were like a corpse, we could get ourselves out of money problems. We wouldn't spend any money because we wouldn't desire to buy anything. What in your life needs to die?

However, when we drive down the same road as the hearse with the dead body, we want to shop in the mall, attend the movies or go relax in a bar. We've got things we want to buy that we think are absolutely necessary. We want things because we're alive.

So what's the answer? We can't be a halfway corpse—half alive and half dead. We're either one or the other. Just so, we can't halfway kill our burning desires to spend money. Think about what that would mean. Would we spend money on the even days of the month but save our money on the odd days? That would never work.

Paul said, "I die daily" (1 Cor. 15:31). By that he meant, "The world has been crucified to me, and I to the world" (Gal. 6:14). When Paul was crucified, he treated the desires of the flesh as if they were dead. He didn't listen to them. That's what we've got to do to our greed—kill it!

The best place to die is at the foot of the Cross. We go to the place where Jesus died for us, and we identify with Him. We die with Jesus: "I have been crucified with Christ; it is no longer I who live, but Christ lives in me" (Gal. 2:20). Though we die to our lust and evil desires, we still have to live in this present world. This means we must do more than *act* as if our lusts are dead—if we have to act like they're dead, that means they're still alive. We must go to the Cross and crucify them.

As we fast in the presence of God, we must weep over our financial irresponsibility. We must ask God's forgiveness, repent and promise the Lord that from now on we will remember that all of our money is His money. Then when our lusts cry out to us to spend money, we recognize and remember that those lusts died with Christ on Calvary.

A Christian should be a new person. If we are Christians, that means we treat our money in a new way. If we are new persons in Jesus Christ, we should spend our money in new ways because we have a new motive in our lives. Obviously, spending our money in a new way means purchasing only those things that God would have us buy.

Paul said, "We were buried with Him through baptism into death, that just as Christ was raised from the dead by the glory of the Father, even so we also should walk in newness of life" (Rom. 6:4). Just as a Christian should walk in newness of life, we must manage our lives with new motives, for a new boss—Jesus

Christ. From now on, we spend only what Jesus tells us to spend.

As we fast, we are continually saying *no* to our appetite. We are continually looking into the face of God. We are learning satisfaction in His presence. We then carry over into everyday financial life the lessons that we learn while fasting.

TAKE-AWAY PRINCIPLES

- God has a faith-based formula for us to get a solution to our money problem.
- The solution to our money problem is based on our walk with God.
- When we fast, we conform ourselves to God's plan for our money.
- The Bible says much about money; we should apply God's Word to our lives.
- A financial breakthrough to our money problem should be tied to our ongoing stewardship.

Note
1. Bankruptcy is a financial solution provided by our American legal system to help individuals deal with debt restructuring and/or debt elimination. Some Christians and Christian institutions have gained protection under bankruptcy laws and have been able to start over again. Some Christian financial counselors feel believers are always obligated to repay their debts, even after they have been eliminated by bankruptcy. Other Christian counselors believe Christians should take advantage of these laws, just as others in our society do. Whether you agree or disagree, many believers have been helped by this temporary protection until they are able to get back on their financial feet.

CHAPTER 7

SATAN AND MONEY

Satan hates God so much that he will use money to destroy God's work and His workers. What did Satan use in his first attempt to destroy the New Testament Church? Money! Acts 5:1-11 tell of a rich husband and wife, leaders in the Church, who were blinded by greed. Ananias and Sapphira were envious of the public acclaim that Barnabas received from Christians when he sold a piece of ground and gave all the proceeds to God. Ananias and Sapphira decided to sell their land as well. They wanted the same cheer from the crowd. However, after they sold their possession, the two of them decided to keep part of the money, while still seeking the public acclaim. Therefore, they let everyone think that they were giving the entire amount of the proceeds of their sale to God.

When Ananias brought the money to the church, Peter said, "Why has Satan filled your heart to lie to the Holy Spirit?" (Acts

5:3). Satan got to Ananias and his wife because they agreed to keep back part of the money, letting everyone believe a lie. Now remember, Satan is called the father of lies (see John 8:44). When Ananias was struck dead because of his lie, young men immediately buried him. Where was Sapphira? Probably out shopping, spending the money they had kept back from God.

When Sapphira came in to the church later, she was confronted with the same sin: "How is it that you have agreed together to test the Spirit of the Lord?" (Acts 5:9). She dropped dead and was taken out by the same burial detail. What was the response? "Great fear came upon all the church and upon all who heard these things" (v. 11). God cleansed the Church, and all the people were afraid to cheat on God or to tell even a small lie about their money. Ananias and Sapphira didn't need to die. They didn't need to sell. They didn't need to give all of it. They didn't need to lie. But they did!

Even unbelievers were influenced by the event. "None of the rest dared join them, but the people esteemed them highly" (v. 13). And many people were converted (see v. 14).

THEY DIDN'T NEED TO DIE

They didn't need to sell.
They didn't need to give all of it.
They didn't need to lie.
But they did!

WANTING TO GET TO GOD THROUGH YOUR MONEY

Although Satan used the surplus of money Ananias and Sapphira received from the sale of their land to tempt them to sin, he tempt-ed another by taking away his money. Job was a rich man. "Also, his possessions were seven thousand sheep, three thousand camels, five hundred yoke of oxen, five hundred female donkeys, and a very large household, so that this man was the greatest of all the people of the East" (Job 1:3). But Job's greatest wealth was not his money; it was his walk with God. "Job . . . was blameless and upright, and one who feared God and shunned evil" (v. 1).

> Satan wants to get to God through your money.

The story is well known that Satan told God that Job would curse Him if God took away Job's money. But even when Job lost all his possessions—everything—he still didn't deny God, blame God or curse God. His life was not wrapped up in money and things. When his health was taken away, his wife wanted him to "curse God and die" (2:9). But even when his wife wanted Job dead, he remained faithful to God. What would you have done?

While the account of Job looks like a story about money, it's not. It's never about money. It's about one man's relationship with God. And our financial problems are not about money. They're about our relationship with God.

> Our money problems are not about money, just as
> our fasting is not about food.

Satan tried to embarrass God by getting Job to deny his faith. The enemy thought he could do it through money. He told God, "Does Job fear God for nothing? . . . You have blessed the work of his hands" (1:9-10). Here was Satan's proposition: "Stretch out Your hand and touch all that he has, and he will surely curse You to Your face!" (v. 11).

Satan hates God, and when he can get to God's workers, Satan gets to God. Notice what Paul said: "The people You forgave for sinning against Your church, I forgave, because Satan gets to us if we have an unforgiving spirit. I forgive them because I live in Christ. I am not ignorant of Satan's devices to get to me" (see 2 Cor. 2:10-11).

TEMPTING GOD'S PEOPLE

Satan doesn't have to try very hard to tempt us with money because there is a natural love within the heart for money and the things that it will buy. Paul reminded us in 1 Timothy 6:10, "The love of money is a root of all kinds of evil."

Some find themselves in a money hole because of their worship of the almighty dollar. How does this happen? Some are slaves to money, and they sacrifice their families, their church time and even their souls to get more of it. This is an addiction called greed, and fasting can help set people free from it.

Some are not addicted to greed; they just want the things that money can buy—luxuries, the latest trinkets or fad purchases. As a result, they are in a money hole, and they need to break their fixation on things. This can be done through prayer and fasting.

Because some people have so little discipline, they spend all their weekly cash, run up debt on their credit cards and then get new credit cards. Next, they try to borrow themselves out of debt. Finally, they try to pray themselves out of debt. But they're in financial bondage because they don't understand freedom in Christ.

SIDETRACKING GOD'S PEOPLE

Satan will use money in an attempt to sidetrack God's people, convincing them to buy "good things" so that they miss the best things in life. Some Christians are fair money managers, so they have enough money to buy all the things in life they want. They've got a recreational vehicle, a boat, extravagant vacations, a cabin at the lake and the latest in televisions, computers, DVDs and other electronic gadgets. They're not in financial debt because, technically, they're able to pay for everything they have. The problem is that their lives are wrapped up in *stuff*, rather than in Jesus Christ.

If Satan can't get us into deep sin or into rebellion against God, then he will try to get us sidetracked with good things. Some Christians complain that they can't put their children in Christian schools because they can't afford tuition, but they're leaning against a $40,000 cabin cruiser in the driveway.

Other Christians give a minimum of 10 percent to God, but they live exorbitantly on the remaining 90 percent. Rather than learning to live a modest lifestyle and seeing how much they can invest in the work of God, they spend excessively on fun, recreation and material things. They are not gripped by fleshly sins or heresy, but at the same time, they're not gripped by Christ. Without realizing it, they're actually in the grips of Satan.

MISDIRECTING FINANCIAL RESOURCES

Satan will bring people into our lives to thwart and misdirect our financial resources away from the work of God. When Satan can't get to us through our carnal nature—the love of money— he'll bring someone else along to destroy our stewardship. This may be a family member who puts a tremendous financial burden on us to divert money away from the work of God. This could be a salesman who wants to sell us additional insurance, stocks or any other item. After all, a salesman's favorite word is "now." If we don't buy right now, we'll miss out. But unless it is truly a life-or-death situation right now, we shouldn't do it. Instead, when we are pressured to make an immediate decision, we should stop and make that decision a matter of prayer. If it's a serious financial investment of money, we should make it a matter of *continued* fasting and prayer.

We also need to watch out for people who travel among the churches with get-rich-quick schemes. They may promise to double our money next year, or they may promise a tremendous retirement in the future. Usually when a financial deal sounds too good to be true—it is.

As we fast and pray about people who make financial offers to us, we must take time to examine the offers carefully. We should commit at least one day to fasting about the proposal. As we do, we should bring several resources to our fast.

- We should fast and pray over all the paperwork related to the investment.
- We should study God's Word as we pray about how to invest money.
- We should study the Bible concerning what God says about investments.

Obviously, we're also going to talk to other Christians whom we respect and trust, as well as others who have invested in the proposed project. Then we need to talk to the respected authorities who deal with the type of investment we're considering. We must do everything we can to find the truth, because the truth will make us free (see John 8:32).

DISRUPTING FINANCIAL SECURITY THROUGH CIRCUMSTANCES AND EXPERIENCES

Satan will bring circumstances and experiences into our lives that will disrupt our financial security and financial spending plans. We never know when medical emergencies or accidents will occur. Satan may inspire some of them, although we know that God is teaching us through these things, working them together for good (see Rom. 8:28). Institutions may collapse and businesses may close. These closings may threaten our financial future and, in turn, disrupt our peace with God. When something happens through theft, financial mismanagement or just unfortunate circumstances, we must turn to God. It's possible that our retirement plans may collapse because God has other plans and wants us to trust Him. Then again, it's possible that Satan has had some part in that collapse.

What do we do when these things happen? Often we lose our present peace and our trust in the future. But perhaps we had our eyes on circumstances and the Dow Jones average, rather than on God. We were not trusting the Lord God of the ages. Sometimes, like a small speck that gets into our eye so that we can't see, money dilutes our vision of God. We don't see His works in our lives, and we forget the principles by which we should be living. It is during those times that we should stop, wait on God and seek His direction.

What is money? Money represents our life. So when the enemy wants to get to us, he comes after our money. He will starve us in an attempt to turn us against God. Or He will give us so much that we'll forget about God entirely. The writer of Proverbs expressed it this way:

Two things I request of You (deprive me not before I die):
Remove falsehood and lies far from me; give me neither
poverty nor riches—feed me with the food allotted to me;
lest I be full and deny You, and say, "Who is the LORD?"
Or lest I be poor and steal, and profane the name of my
God (30:7-9).

TAKE-AWAY PRINCIPLES

- Satan will tempt us through money.
- Satan can get us in trouble when we spend too much or we spend unwisely.
- Satan can tempt us by taking away our money.

EPILOGUE

When investigative reporters from the *Washington Post* were trying to find the truth about President Nixon, they were told to follow the money trail. When the IRS wants to catch those who cheat on their income taxes, they follow the money trail. What does God do when trying to determine our spirituality? He follows our money trail.

Let's be quick to point out that proper management of our money will not make us spiritual. But if we are properly related to Christ and growing in Him, it follows that we will properly manage our money.

When God follows our money trail, it's not a matter of how much we have—whether we are rich or poor—it's what we do with what we have. God is looking for faithfulness. If we've been faithful with our money, we'll hear Him say, "Well done, good and faithful servant" (Matt. 25:21).

But some believers have financial problems through no fault of their own. Businesses collapse, accidents occur, illnesses attack, and the affected believers can't handle the financial fallout. What can they do in that sort of situation? God still answers prayer to meet the needs—including the financial needs—of His children. So we may need to fast and pray for a financial breakthrough.

There are also Christian ministries and workers who have gigantic financial needs from week to week, as well as occasional crisis situations. They too have the promise that God will be with them and answer them when they pray and fast in His name. If you are in this situation, bring your requests to God and let Him take care of you.

RECOMMENDED READING

Blue, Ron. *Generous Living*. **Grand Rapids, MI: Zondervan, 1997.**

Financial advisor Ron Blue explains why an openhanded spirit is the key to freedom, contentment and joy. He helps us start cultivating a generous lifestyle right where we are and shows us what happens when we become givers. *Generous Living* points us beyond guilt-induced giving and shows us the true Bible-based way to give effectively, joyfully and wisely.

_____. *Master Your Money*. **Rev. ed. Nashville, TN: Thomas Nelson, 1997.**

Ron Blue combines the Bible's timeless teachings on stewardship and responsibility with up-to-date advice on financial management and cash control. New, easy-to-follow charts as well as updated worksheets and a handy glossary of terms make this a step-by-step plan for financial freedom.

Blue, Ron, and Blue, J. *A Woman's Guide to Financial Peace of Mind.* **Colorado Springs, CO: Focus on the Family, 2001.**
A woman's season of life strongly influences her financial priorities and concerns. This book looks carefully at each season and offers clear, practical help for meeting its challenges, while offering keys to financial success in any season.

Blue, Ron; Blue, J.; and Berndt, J. *Money Talks and So Can We.* **Grand Rapids, MI: Zondervan, 1999.**
Financial expert Ron Blue and wife, Judy, insist that marital problems are not about money but about the failure to communicate on different issues such as finances. This book shows husbands and wives how to operate as a team, overcoming individual weaknesses and uniting strengths to cultivate vision and prosperity in marriage.

Burkett, Larry. *Complete Financial Guide for Couples.* **Colorado Springs, CO: Cook Communications, 1993.**
Without a solid financial and spiritual foundation on which to base sound decisions, problems—and not just money problems—tend to multiply in a marriage. Best-selling author Burkett steers young marrieds—as well as those about to marry—around the pitfalls that result from mishandling money. This book also includes advice on establishing a workable budget.

_____. *Debt-Free Living: How to Get Out of Debt (And Stay Out).* **Chicago: Moody Press, 2001.**
Designed to help individuals understand the origin of most financial troubles, *Debt-Free Living* provides a means to escape

the "debt cycle." Best-selling author Larry Burkett warns readers about the kinds of credit to avoid, while suggesting viable alternatives.

_____. *The Family Financial Workbook: A Family Budgeting Guide*. **Chicago: Moody Press, 2000.**
A budget is not a financial straitjacket for the monetarily insane. It's a plan of action. This book shows families how to get a grip on their finances and break free from debt.

_____. *The Financial Guide for the Single Parent.*
Chicago: Moody Press, 1997.
Whether man or woman, divorced, widowed or never wed, single parents face unique financial problems. By sharing biblically based advice, financial expert Larry Burkett helps readers make a budget, find housing, buy a car and deal with court battles.

_____. *How to Manage Your Money: An In-Depth Bible Study on Personal Finances*. **Chicago: Moody Press, 2000.**
Not to be confused with his workbook on family budgeting, this book by Larry Burkett puts the focus on the management of individual finances. The need for such a book, he asserts, is implicit in the Bible itself, where, he says, he has found 700 direct references to money.

Not only does the author offer guidance on understanding God's will in finances, but he also offers plenty of practical advice on avoiding debt, accumulating money and managing investments.

_____. *Larry Burkett's Bill Organizer.*
Chicago: Moody Press, 1999.
This expanding file of durable green transparent plastic contains 12 tabbed pockets that can be customized easily to orga-

nize bills, either by category or due date. Preprinted stickers and ledger sheets for tracking payments are included. Also included with the bill organizer is Larry's helpful audiocassette "Taking Charge of Your Credit Card."

_____. *Learning for Life: Your Child and Money: A Family Activity Book*. **Chicago: Moody Press, 2000.**
This book enables parents to give their children a debt-free future, a nice home, good cars and an abundant retirement. It even helps readers assure college educations and nice weddings for their grandchildren.

About the Author

Elmer L. Towns is dean of the School of Religion
at Liberty University in Lynchburg, Virginia, where he teaches
the 2,000-member Pastor's Sunday School class at Thomas
Road Baptist Church. He is a Gold Medallion Award-winning
author whose books include *Fasting for Spiritual Breakthrough*
and *My Father's Names*. Elmer Towns and his wife,
Ruth, have three grown children.

etowns@elmertowns.com

ALSO BY
ELMER L. TOWNS

The Names of Jesus

My Father's Names

The Names of the Holy Spirit

Fasting for Spiritual Breakthrough

*Praying the Lord's Prayer for
Spiritual Breakthrough*

My Angel Named Herman

Praying the 23rd Psalm

What Every Sunday School Teacher Should Know

Prayer Partners

More Ways To Break Through
with Fasting and Prayer

Fasting for Spiritual Breakthrough
A Guide to Nine Biblical Fasts
Elmer L. Towns
Paperback
ISBN 08307.18397

Fasting Can Change Your Life
True Stories of How God Has used Fasting in the Lives of Today's Christian Leaders
Jerry Falwell and *Elmer L. Towns*
Paperback
ISBN 08307.21975

Biblical Meditation for Spiritual Breakthrough
Cultivating a Deeper Relationship with the Lord Through Biblical Meditation
Elmer L. Towns
Paperback
ISBN 08307.23609

Fasting for Spiritual Breakthrough Study Guide
A Guide to Nine Biblical Fasts
Elmer L. Towns
Paperback
ISBN 08307.18478

Praying the Lord's Prayer for Spiritual Breakthrough
Praying the Lord's Prayer Daily As a Pathway Into His Presence
Elmer L. Towns
Paperback
ISBN 08307.20421

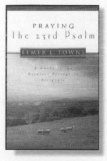

Praying the 23rd Psalm
"The Lord is my Shepherd; I shall not want."
Elmer L. Towns
Paperback
ISBN 08307.27760

More Ways Elmer Towns Can Help You and Your Church

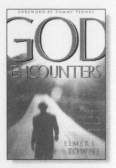

God Encounters
To Touch God and Be Touched by Him
Elmer L. Towns
Paperback
ISBN 08307.23366

My Father's Names
The Old Testament Names of God and How They Can Help You Know Him More Intimately
Elmer L. Towns
Paperback
ISBN 08307.14472

Prayer Partners
How to Increase the Power and Joy of Your Prayer Life by Praying with Others
Elmer L. Towns
Paperback
ISBN 08307.29348

The Son
He Was Sent to Save the World
Elmer L. Towns
Paperback
ISBN 08307.24281

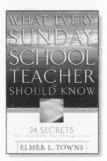

What Every Sunday School Teacher Should Know
24 Secrets That Can Help You Change Lives
Elmer L. Towns
Mass
ISBN 08307.28740

The Year-Round Church Event Book
A Step-by-Step Guide to Planning and Promoting Successful Events
Elmer L. Towns and *Dr. Stan Toler*
Reproducible Manual
ISBN 08307.20405

043740